A Concise History of Portugal

This concise, illustrated history of Portugal offers an introduction to the people and culture of the country and its empire, and to its search for economic modernisation, political stability and international partnership.

It is the first modern account of Portugal's history to be written in English since the days of dictatorship. A short introduction to Portugal's classical, Islamic and Hispanic history culminates in the revolution of 1640. The book then studies the effects of the vast wealth mined from Portuguese Brazil, the growth of the wine trade and the evolution of close ties with England, Portugal's 'oldest ally'. The Portuguese Revolution of 1820 to 1851 created a liberal monarchy, but in 1910 the king was overthrown and, by 1926, had been replaced by a dictatorship which tried to overcome Portugal's poverty by building a new empire in Africa. In 1975 Portugal withdrew from its African colonies and turned north to become a democratic member of the European Community in 1986.

David Birmingham visited Portugal as a summer student in Coimbra while training as a historian at the University of Ghana in 1960. His first major book was a history of early modern Angola and he has since co-edited a three-volume history of Central Africa. He has also written biography, with a study of Kwame Nkrumah, local history, with a book on a Swiss village, and thematic history, with a work on nationalism. The present *Concise History* was researched during the years which followed the fall of Portugal's dictators in 1974, and it has since become the standard single-volume work. This second edition brings the story up to date and the revised bibliography discusses the current state of historical writing on Portugal.

DAVID BIRMINGHAM is Emeritus Professor of Modern History in the University of Kent at Canterbury.

CAMBRIDGE CONCISE HISTORIES

A Concise History of Portugal

CAMBRIDGE CONCISE HISTORIES

This is a new series of illustrated 'concise histories' of selected individual countries, intended both as university and college textbooks and as general historical introductions for general readers, travellers and members of the business community.

First titles in the series:

A Concise History of Germany
MARY FULBROOK

A Concise History of Greece
RICHARD CLOGG

A Concise History of France
ROGER PRICE

A Concise History of Britain, 1707–1795
W. A. SPECK

A Concise History of Portugal
DAVID BIRMINGHAM

A Concise History of Italy
CHRISTOPHER DUGGAN

A Concise History of Bulgaria
RICHARD CRAMPTON

A Concise History of South Africa
ROBERT ROSS

A Concise History of Brazil
BORIS FAUSTO

A Concise History of Mexico
BRIAN HAMNETT

A Concise History of Australia
STUART MACINTYRE

Other titles are in preparation

A Concise History of Portugal

SECOND EDITION

DAVID BIRMINGHAM

PUBLISHED BY THE PRESS SYNDICATE OF THE UNIVERSITY OF CAMBRIDGE
The Pitt Building, Trumpington Street, Cambridge, United Kingdom

CAMBRIDGE UNIVERSITY PRESS
The Edinburgh Building, Cambridge CB2 2RU, UK
40 West 20th Street, New York, NY 10011–4211, USA
477 Williamstown Road, Port Melbourne, VIC 3207, Australia
Ruiz de Alarcón 13, 28014 Madrid, Spain
Dock House, The Waterfront, Cape Town 8001, South Africa

http://www.cambridge.org

First published 1993
Reprinted 4 times
Second edition 2003

Printed in the United Kingdom at the University Press, Cambridge

Typeface Sabon 10/13 pt.   *System* LATEX 2ε   [TB]

A catalogue record for this book is available from the British Library

Library of Congress Cataloguing in Publication data
Birmingham, David
A concise history of Portugal / David Birmingham.
p.   cm. – (Cambridge concise histories)
Includes bibliographical references.
ISBN 0 521 83004 4 – ISBN 0 521 53686 3 (pbk.)
1. Portugal – History. 1. Title 11. Series
DG538.B57   1993
946.9 – dc20   92-33824 CIP

ISBN 0 521 83004 4 hardback
ISBN 0 521 53686 3 paperback

For
Alberto Romão Dias
and
Jill R. Dias

CONTENTS

ILLUSTRATIONS

MAPS

Map 1   Portugal

Introduction

Portugal is one of history's most successful survivors. It is but a small country whose population rose slowly from one million to nine million over eight hundred years. In that time it acquired a political and cultural autonomy within Europe. It also made its mark on every corner of the globe through colonisation, emigration and commerce. Unlike the more prosperous Catalonia it succeeded in escaping from Spanish captivity in the seventeenth century. Unlike the equally dynamic Scotland it was not politically absorbed by its English economic patron in the eighteenth century. Unlike the middle-ranking kingdoms of Naples or Bavaria it was not cannibalised in the unification of the great nineteenth-century land empires of Europe. Unlike Germany and Italy it did not lose its African colonies in either the First or the Second World War. And unlike other farming countries such as Ireland or Denmark it remained outside the European Economic Community until the 1980s.

But Portugal was more than a tenacious survivor in modern history. It was also a pioneer in many of the historical developments of the European world. Portuguese Christians of the middle ages, with a little help from English mercenaries, fought bloodily against Portuguese Muslims to dominate the western rim of Europe by the thirteenth century. The Portuguese created Europe's first 'modern' nation state whose frontiers have not changed since the fall of the old Muslim 'Kingdom of the West' in the Algarve. A century later they pioneered the concept of overseas colonisation on the islands of the Atlantic. By the sixteenth century they had found the sea lane to Asia. Portugal's pepper empire may have been short-lived, but it opened the way for the great trading empires of The Netherlands and Britain which followed in its train. In America, Portugal's conquest of the Brazils outstripped in size the thirteen British colonies which were to become the United States of America. Moreover the flow of Portuguese gold from the Brazilian highlands was an important ingredient in fuelling the European industrial revolution which began in eighteenth-century Britain.

It was not only in its overseas enterprises that Portugal led the way. It was also a pioneer in the search for new forms of social organisation in Europe. Portuguese liberalism sought to free the country from excessive clericalism and pave the way for democracy and humanitarianism. Portugal was one of the first Old World nations to adopt a republican form of government in the French mode. At the same time Portugal had to struggle to dominate its less-than-bountiful environment. In the seventeenth century the exchequer was constantly stretched by the demands of naval warfare to protect Portuguese independence and recover the Atlantic colonies. In the eighteenth century monumental projects of public works were undertaken and prestigious royal palaces were built far in excess of the architectural expectations of a small agrarian country. In the nineteenth century the profits of the last phase of the African slave trade and the remittances of millions of migrants to the New World enabled Portugal to sustain a cultured middle class in elegant Victorian style. The historian is left with a rich harvest of questions as to how so small a nation achieved so much over so many centuries.

One constant refrain of modern Portuguese history is the search for economic modernisation. From the earliest days of Portuguese independence, when the rebellion against the Spanish captivity broke out in 1640, Portugal was economically linked to its naval protector, England. Not surprisingly it therefore aspired to emulate England in the growth and diversification of its economic activities. In particular Portugal sought to escape from the 'underdevelopment' trap which constantly drove it to supply raw materials and buy finished manufactures. The attempt to initiate an industrial revolution was undertaken four times, in four different centuries, with varying degrees of success. In the seventeenth century, when the wars of independence were over, the landowners and the burghers engaged in a fierce struggle over the development of a woollen textile industry. The landowners won, and the burghers' interests were diverted to the new-found opportunities of Brazil. Not until the Brazilian gold ran dry in the late eighteenth century did industrialisation again become a priority of the Portuguese government. But manufacturing could not compete with the quality wine trade as a source of foreign exchange and vines came to be almost the monoculture of Portugal after the decline of Brazilian mining. The third attempt at a manufacturing revolution, and the creation of import substitution industries, occurred in the late nineteenth century when the wine trade dipped and foreign competition stole a march on Portugal. The rise of mechanised industry was sufficiently important to create an urban proletariat which took a new role in the affairs of the country and helped to proclaim the republic in 1910. But the world recession of 1930, and a long backward-looking dictatorship which idealised peasant poverty and which protected a highly privileged oligarchy, brought a generation of stagnation. The fourth industrial leap only occurred in the 1960s when Portugal gained some benefit from the world division of labour as multinational companies sought out the most disciplined and underpaid labour markets as openings for the transfer of factories from high-cost, heavily unionised, areas of traditional industrial production. At the same period domestic industrial entrepreneurs began to make belated use of Portugal's African colonies, and of its close access to mainland Europe, to build up textiles, plastics, shipbuilding and light engineering. By 1986, when Portugal finally entered the European Community, the process of modernisation was well under way at the fourth attempt.

Finding a suitable chronology into which to divide the modern history of Portugal presents a variety of options. The seventeenth century was essentially the age of nationalism. The escape from Spain began in 1640 and was finally acknowledged in 1668 after a generation of desultory warmongering on the fringes of the great wars of national identity in early modern Europe. But nationalism required recognition and protection from sympathetic allies, and these had to be paid for. One asset which Portugal had was a royal princess, Catherine of Braganza, who was sent to England with a huge dowry when a more prestigious French suitor could not be arranged. But a dynastic alliance was not sufficient to ensure national survival and the constant support of English naval power. In 1703 the Luso-Britannic alliance, which had its roots in the fourteenth-century ex-change of wine for woollen cloth, was re-enforced by the famous, or some would say infamous, treaty signed by John Methuen. In some respects the Methuen Treaty made Portugal a 'neo-colonial' client of Britain, but the treaty was not quite as unequal as might appear and became a permanent factor in guaranteeing, albeit at a price, the nationalism which Portugal had won in the seventeenth century.

The history of the eighteenth century is dominated by the Lisbon earthquake of 1755, probably the only episode of Portuguese history which has been etched on to the folk memory of European culture. Yet the eighteenth century was one of spectacular ostentation as the church, the crown and the nobility vied with one another in building chapels and palaces gilded with the gold of Brazil. The Braganzas were thought by contemporary opinion to be the wealthiest family in the world. One of the side chapels of the church of São Roque was built of precious marble in Rome, that it might be blessed by the Pope before being dismantled and reassembled piece by piece in Lisbon. The great palace-convent of Mafra was built in monumental Spanish style, and the Lisbon aqueduct brought water to the city on Roman-type stone columns nearly two hundred feet high. But the wealth faded after the earthquake, and Portugal entrusted its destiny to one of the great enlightened despots of the eighteenth century, the Marquis of Pombal. After serving a long diplomatic apprenticeship in London and Vienna he struggled to modernise the country, freeing the Jews from church persecution, abolishing slavery outside the colonies, curtailing the power of the nobility, encouraging the rise of the bourgeoisie, enhancing the profits of the British wine trade and reforming state methods of administration and finance.

The eighteenth century came to a close in two stages. In stage one Napoleon's armies invaded Portugal and the royal family with its thousands of retainers fled, as they had occasionally thought to do during previous crises, to their richer transatlantic dominions at Rio de Janeiro. The armies of Wellington promptly counter-invaded and delayed for ten years the Portuguese access to the new revolutionary ideas of the nineteenth century. The Portuguese Revolution did not therefore break out until 1820. It was no less vigorous for all that and, like the French Revolution before it, went through phases of constitutional radicalism, reactionary repression, civil war, popular uprising and urban terror. By 1851, when the revolution was over, Portugal had been significantly transformed. The old eighteenth-century bourgeoisie had turned itself into the new nobility. Its leaders had dissolved the monasteries, distributed the church lands, sold the crown estates, founded a string of new aristocratic titles and created a parliamentary system with a highly restricted property franchise for the 'commons' and a British-style second house of parliament for the lords. The new barons launched half a century of increasingly immobile political stability after thirty eventful years of evolution.

The Victorian age in Portugal was reigned over by the ubiquitous house of Saxe-Coburg. King-Consort Ferdinand and his sons were patrons of the arts. The Lisbon botanical gardens were admired by Baedeker as the finest in Europe. The beau monde went to the Maria II Opera House to see and be seen. Lisbon was linked to Paris in a fever of railway-age speculative investment. The city built a network of funiculars, tramways and public elevators with the engineering help of the famous Eiffel. The role of government was broadened by vigorous programmes of public works. The only hiccups occurred when the price of wine dipped, as in 1870 and in 1890. Portugal tried to counter these losses by a return to the imperial past. Efforts to build a third empire, this time not in Asia or America but in Africa, were temporarily thwarted by the cautious limitations of Portuguese speculative investors and by the ambitions of rival British imperialists in Central Africa. This was not, however, before the appetite of popular Portuguese nationalism for colonial ventures had been whetted. Colonial conquests created folk heroes and colonial failures helped to bring the long Victorian age of stability to an end.

The age of Victorian liberalism came to an end in three stages. In the first stage, in 1890, Portugal came into collision with Britain in Africa and had to withdraw its claims to the Zambezi heartlands in favour of Cecil Rhodes. The national loss of face discredited the government and brought the royal dynasty into disrepute. Within twenty years Portuguese republicans, both democrats and anarchists, had toppled the monarchy and declared a liberal republic in 1910. The republic was no more able to win wealth from the colonies, or to pursue a foreign policy independent of Great Britain, or to satisfy the legitimate demands of the rising proletariat and of the lower middle class, than had been the bourgeois monarchy. It too was toppled, but this time by right-wing Catholic rebels from the senior cadres of the army. The coup of 1926 ushered in a fourth and last stage of modern Portuguese history. After the national mercantilism of the seventeenth century, and absolutist imperialism of the eighteenth century and the liberal monarchy of the nineteenth century, the twentieth century became an era of authoritarian conservatism.

The army rebels of 1926 at first had no success at all in advancing their partisan interests. Within two years they sold out to a staunch Catholic layman called Salazar, a homburg-hatted lecturer in economics at Coimbra university law faculty, who guaranteed to finance the well-being and social prestige of the armed forces in return for a dictatorial free hand in running the country. This unholy alliance, forged in the early years of European fascism, brought Portugal a period of stern economic recession, authoritarian police government and polarised social stratification. Only after forty years of bitter monetarist medicine did any economic liberalisation begin to take place in the 1960s. It was still another ten years before democracy was restored, after a brief revolutionary upheaval in 1974–5, and only after that was Portugal accepted into the institutions of the European Community.

In attempting an overview of the significance of Portuguese history it is difficult to decide whether the most distinctive feature is the isolated traditionalism of the countryside or the close integration of Lisbon city into world developments. Having once stood tall at the apex of the triangle linking Africa, Europe and Latin America, Portugal gained its autonomy by a series of dramatic breaks with its main correspondents. It broke with Spain in 1640, with Brazil in 1822, with Britain in 1890 and with Africa in 1974. The isolation of most of Portugal was striking and it was almost insulated from the French Revolution for a whole generation. Portugal also remained on the fringe of the industrial revolution despite the aspirations of its liberal élite. More strikingly still Portugal was insulated from the transformations of the Second World War: social values of almost Edwardian conservatism continued to prevail until the 1960s. Despite the country's political and social isolation, Lisbon and Oporto tried to follow developments in Europe and the ideologies of Spanish political change usually spread quite rapidly to the Portuguese capital. At the opposite end of Europe Portugal showed illuminating parallels with Scotland, a country of fishermen, shepherds and farmers which fell under the economic sway of England, and also with Ireland, a country of predominantly poor Catholic peasants. Both Celtic nations emulated Portugal in sending large communities of migrants to the Americas where all three left profound cultural imprints on the societies of the New World.

The cultural individuality of Portugal has attracted many excellent observers and scholars, both national and foreign. The observations of British visitors to Portugal over the centuries were collected by Rose Macaulay in a fascinating volume of wry perceptiveness. The historian of empire *par excellence* was Charles Boxer, whose books brought Portugal to world attention. His contemporary in the field of economic history was Magalhães Godinho whose great works were initially researched in exile in France. Another distinguished exile, Oliveira Marques, returned from the United States to pioneer a new vein of biographical studies before embarking on the large-scale entrepreneurial editing of volumes ranging from fifteenth-century Atlantic colonisation to the republican empire in twentieth-century Africa. After the revolution of 1974 Portuguese historians were able to catch up with new intellectual fashions, especially in social and industrial history. British traditions of scholarship influenced the works of José Cutileiro, Vasco Pulido Valente, Jill Dias and Jaime Reis. The role of empire was soberly reassessed by Joseph Miller in the United States and by Gervase Clarence-Smith in Britain. Meanwhile in Portugal the thirst for knowledge was partly satisfied by a richly illustrated six-volume serial history edited by José Hermano Saraiva.

Since the appearance of the first edition of this book a great deal of new work has been published in English, in Portuguese and in French and the book itself is now available in both Portuguese and Spanish. A selection of new books, together with a few lines of commentary on each, is appended to this second edition. More audaciously a few new pages have been devoted to Portugal since 1990 despite all warnings that historians should not press their noses too flat against the windowpane.

Among the new works there are several massive, multi-volume
compilations in which dozens of Portugal's best post-revolutionary
historians have collaborated to produce not only new surveys of
Portugal and of its empire but also revisionist interpretations of the
past which are refreshingly radical. One of the innovations of the
first edition of this concise history was an attempt to shed an unfash-
ionably positive light on the social achievements of Portugal both
during the nineteenth-century era of liberalism and during the first
republic of the early twentieth century. This glimmer of new perception has since burst into life in the fifth volume of José Mattoso's
História de Portugal which analyses the long era of academic denigration from which modern Portuguese history suffered throughout
the dictatorship of 1926 to 1974, a denigration which rather surprisingly infected much foreign writing on Portugal.

The new historiography does more than merely challenge nega-
tive stereotypes of Portugal. It also sheds fresh light on the myths
which long sustained, and in some cases still sustain, the self-image
of Portugal's patriots and politicians. Throughout the Salazar dictatorship Prince Henry, who had previously acquired heroic status in
Victorian England as the so-called 'navigator', was portrayed as the
embodiment of Portuguese greatness and the impoverished post-war
government of Salazar spent a small fortune on erecting a massive
stone monument in his honour at the entrance to Lisbon harbour.
Revisionists who tried to explore the realities beneath the spin were
accused of 'regicide' but alternative interpretations of the age of exploration and exploitation gradually saw the light and culminated
in Peter Russell's fine biography of the prince.

When in 2002 Portugal completed its entry into the European
Union by adopting the European currency its politicians still needed
patriotic heroes whom they could hero-worship to preserve a sense
of national identity. They were particularly prone to admire Vasco
da Gama after whom a new eight-kilometre bridge across the mighty
Tagus was named five centuries after his tiny fleet had slipped down-
stream on the first European sea voyage to India. Such was the
admiral's historical status that Portuguese statesmen were initially
discomforted when an Indian economic historian, Sanjay Subrahmanyam, wondered aloud whether seamen from so remote and tiny
a kingdom as Portugal could really have created economic waves

among 300 million Asians or whether Vasco da Gama and his successors were little more than drops in the ocean. Open debate, however, had become respectable in the democratic Portugal now rising from the ashes of late European fascism. The new historians who revisited the middle ages, who brought Portugal's art and music into the light, who analysed the roots of their own recent revolution, were therefore bold enough to tackle the great themes of empire with vigorous brush strokes. Scholarship rode high in Portugal.

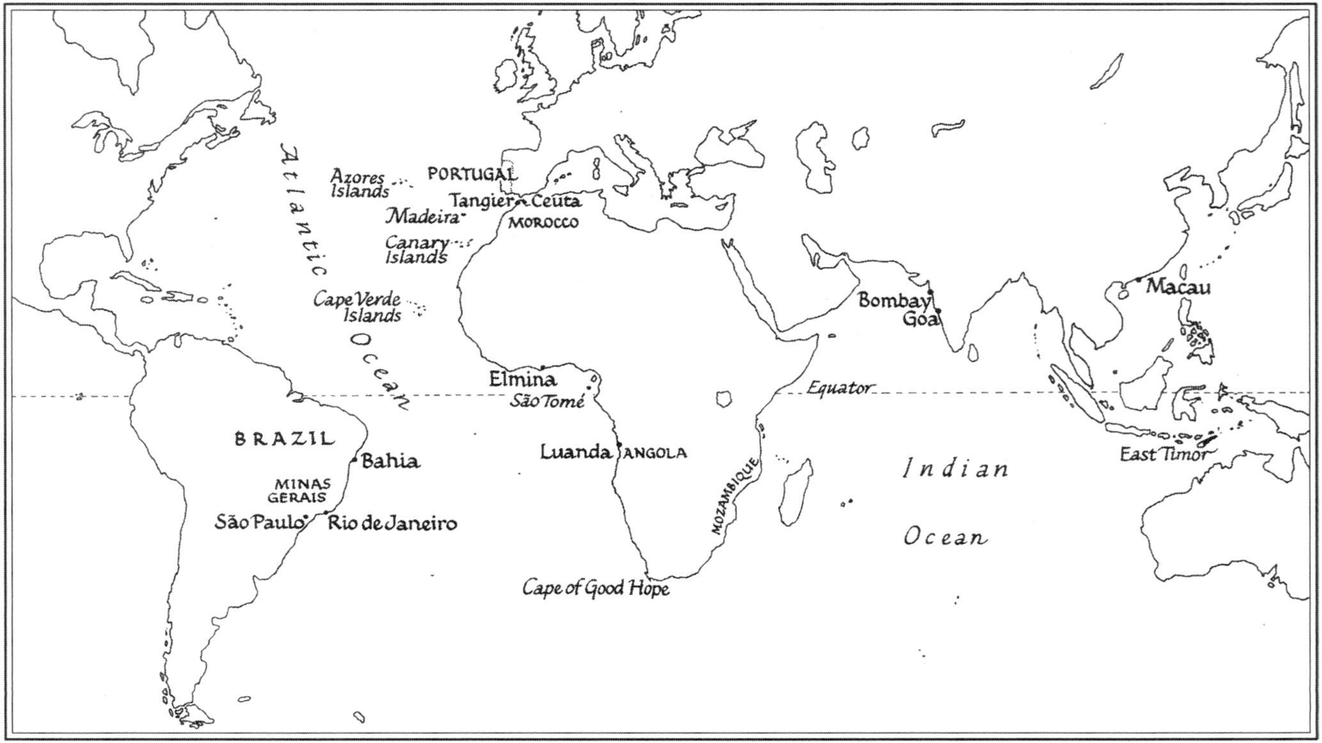

Map 2 Portugal overseas

The following place names appear on the map:

Macau

East Timor

Bombay, Goa

Indian Ocean

Equator

MOZAMBIQUE

Luanda, ANGOLA

Elmina

São Tomé

Cape of Good Hope

PORTUGAL

Tangier, Ceuta

Madeira

MOROCCO

Azores Islands

Canary Islands

Cape Verde Islands

Atlantic Ocean

Bahia

BRAZIL

MINAS GERAIS

São Paulo, Rio de Janeiro

1

Peoples, cultures and colonies

The making of modern Portugal began with the revolution of 1640 and a twenty-eight-year war with Spain. The people of Portugal are of course very much older than the modern state and their history is long and rich. Indeed the medieval kingdom of Portugal is sometimes described as Europe's earliest surviving polity. The cultural roots of Portuguese society go back yet further. Stone Age men and women roamed over western Iberia and even if they did not prosper at least they gave their deceased leaders proper megalithic burials. Neolithic Portugal experimented with the rearing of domestic, or semi-domestic, animals and with the taming of cereal plants; it also developed the marine harvesting of fish which was to become a permanent source of nutrition and economic well-being over the centuries. Portuguese art evolved from stone beads and bone carvings to the ornamentation of early crockery, a craft which has been carried forward to present times. The relatively open frontier on the north and east allowed migrants to come and go bringing each new facet of human technology including copper working, bronze casting and ultimately the making of iron tools. The age of metals also introduced the fashioning of costly jewellery, and the search for gold, both at home and abroad, ran like a fine thread through the subsequent history of Portugal.

During the Iron Age Portuguese culture was regularly enriched by new peoples and ideas from the outer world of Europe, the Mediterranean and Africa. The old Celts, linguistically related to the Bretons and the Welsh, came overland seeking opportunities to farm and settle. Family structure in northern Portugal, and the organisation of villages, derived from Celtic experience. The Celts were also an important source of artistic influence and their musical traditions based on the bagpipes were carried down the ages. In coastal areas colonising influences were brought by sea traders from the Phoenician cities of the Levant. The mines of Portugal, like those of Cornwall, enriched the 'civilisations' of the Mediterranean. Phoenician mariners were succeeded by Greeks and Carthaginians who also left their stamp on the harbours and beaches of the Atlantic shore. Long-distance merchants introduced a shipbuilding technology and a taste for imported wines in jars to supplement the local beers. The greatest colonisers of Portuguese antiquity, however, were the Romans. They colonised both the interior and the seashore.

In the second century before Christ the Romans, having defeated their Carthaginian rivals in western Iberia, set about attempting the conquest of the Lusitanians, later to be known as the Portuguese, in eastern Iberia. After more than 100 years of costly fighting the Roman republic sent Julius Caesar to overcome the ongoing resistance in the central highlands of Portugal. With an army of 15,000 men he crossed the mountains, reached the Atlantic, and fought his way north into the Douro valley. He found 'Portugal' sufficiently prosperous to supply the loot necessary to satisfy his creditors back in Rome. Forty years later the legions completed the bloody 'pacification' of north-western Iberia and four centuries of intellectual and economic Romanisation began to transform the life of the Lusitanian peoples. A strategic highroad was built between the great harbour at Lisbon and the fertile north which was not bettered until the age of rail 2,000 years later. The great rivers were bridged in stone with such engineering skill that some public works stand to this day. Even greater architectural elegance was displayed in the arched aqueducts which carried water across the parched southern plain. At the heart of the country the Roman city of Conimbriga flourished not far from the future medieval city of Coimbra.

Roman colonisation, whether by immigrants from Italy or by retired conscripts who had served their time in the legions, was so intense and so prolonged that the language of the people was Latinised. Equally pervasively the Roman pattern of urban law and

1 Roman architecture brought not only mosaic-paved villas and marble temples to 'Lusitania', but also important civil engineering projects to supply cities such as Evora with water.

administration was adopted. Cities gained financial and juridical rights and responsibilities of lasting complexity. Important towns such as Mértola on the Guadiana River minted their own coins. Municipal government became the linchpin of Portugal's political system. It was also the form of control which the Portuguese carried around the world when they began their own colonising ventures a thousand years after the Romans had ceased to rule the ancient world. Outside of the towns Roman villas became the focus of great landed estates, known in a later age as 'latifundia'. Some of the Roman estates of the southern plains spread out over ten thousand and more acres where client subjects and purchased slaves farmed olives and vines, wheat and rye, figs and cherries. In addition to their crops and cattle some villas along the Tagus River became known for breeding prized Lusitanian horses. The wealthiest owners of villas commissioned fine mosaics on their patios, built hot baths for their guest suites, and owned private temples for their funeral services. Meanwhile their servants and concubines fed on broad bean soup and millet porridge.

The industries of Portuguese antiquity related to the demands of Roman civilisation. Quarries were developed to supply building blocks, paving slabs and fine-grained stone for carved inscriptions. Portugal even quarried some of the marble used for the finest buildings. Opencast mines of gold and lead in the north and of copper and iron in the south were owned by the state and managed by carefully supervised contractors. To limit smuggling and tax evasion anyone caught transporting metals during the hours of darkness was subject to a heavy fine. The workforce consisted exclusively of slaves, a mode of production that was to survive in Portugal until the eighteenth century. On the south coast and around the estuary of the Sado River the main industry was fish conservation. Portuguese tuna paste had been developed as a relish by the Phoenicians, was widely appreciated in classical Athens and became a staple export of the Roman 'Algarve'. The curing of fish required large quantities of salt which was panned around the coasts of Portugal. Fish drying, like ceramics and textiles, was a Roman industry that remained one of the anchors of the Portuguese economy into modern times. But perhaps the most lasting legacy of Rome was the artistic tradition of carved tombs, of marble sculptures, of mosaic pavements, all of

2 Fishing from small open boats has been one of Portugal's major industries and has provided scenes typical from
Carthaginian times to the present day.

which survived to be adapted and imitated through the dark ages
and beyond.

The Germanic invasions which transformed the Roman empire
had their impact on Portugal as elsewhere. Germans settled in the
north of Portugal cheek by jowl with the Romanised Lusitanians. In

many ways the new Germans tried to maintain Roman traditions, imitating their currency for instance. One group of immigrants created a fifth-century kingdom whose capital was established at Braga. The international affiliation of the Braga kingdom may have been to the Byzantine empire of the east, but its autonomy and alliances were not sufficiently mighty to resist incorporation into a wider Germanic empire of Iberia, the kingdom of the Visigoths. Although Gothic domination lasted throughout the seventh century in Portugal, the legal, cultural and economic impact was muted and the capital with its glittering finery lay far away at Toledo in Spain. In many respects the Germanic period in Portugal tends to be better remembered by historians as an interlude between the half millennium of Roman high culture which preceded it and the half millennium of Islamic high culture which followed. One Germanic legacy, however, did survive. That was a strengthened Christianity. The new Mediterranean religion had begun to spread to Portugal in late Roman times, but it was the Germanic princes who gave it a new thrust. The city of Braga became the premier bishopric of Portugal while that of Toledo became the senior ecclesiastical see in Spain. Christianity in Iberia survived five hundred years of Islamic overrule.

The Islamisation of Portugal began late in the first Muslim century. Between 710 and 732 of the Christian calendar Arab armies and their Berber camp-followers from North Africa crossed Iberia and invaded France. They brought with them a new flowering of Mediterranean civilisation. Their capital was to be the wealthy metropolis of Córdoba where the great mosque stretched out under a thousand marble pillars and looked down on the old Roman bridge over the Guadalquivir River. Far to the west Islamisation led to the conversion of a large proportion of the population of Portugal. Old Roman temples were adapted or rebuilt to make new mosques. Christian and Jewish minorities who held fast to their faith were tolerated but Islam became the religion of the people. Only in the far north, where Germanic influence had been strongest, did Islam fail to penetrate as the Christian chiefdoms held out against the imperial might of Córdoba. In the rest of the country up and thrusting young Portuguese left their homes in the west to seek their fortunes as administrators and merchants in the great Muslim cities. In old age they returned full of memories to their villages to grow pumpkins and write pastoral poetry in Arabic verse. The tradition of

emigration and of wistful longing for the idyllic charms of one's native land was already well established in ninth-century Portugal, five
hundred years before Camões wrote his poems about the homesick
Portuguese of India.

Science and learning were among the most profound contribu-
tions which Muslim scholars brought to Portugal. The old Greek
philosophers and mathematicians were rediscovered through the
medium of Arabic translations of the classics. Astrolabes and com-
passes were introduced to facilitate open-sea navigation and map
making. Muslim experience in shipbuilding for the high seas of the
Indian Ocean rather than the quieter Mediterranean was adapted
to suit Atlantic conditions. Arabic technical terms were adopted not
only in naval architecture but also in domestic architecture. Brick
pavings, roofed chimneys and tiled walls became a permanent feature of Portuguese homes. Muslim tiles were geometrically decorated but in later centuries Christians used tiles to build up large
and complex murals depicting heroic episodes of history and scenes
of everyday life. In Muslim Portugal the vernacular language remained Latinised, but technical terms for plants and tools, weights
and measures, carts and harnesses were borrowed from Arabic. The
greatest economic impact of Muslim culture was felt in agriculture.
Irrigation was improved and extended as huge water wheels were
built to lift water from the rivers to the fields. The mechanisation
of corn milling spread in place of the labour-intensive pounding of
mortars. In Muslim Lisbon the city was commended by the geog-
rapher Idrisi for its hot public baths and its good sanitation. Social
life was dominated by music and dancing and the display of fine
costumes. Long after the government of Portugal had changed from
Muslim rule to Christian rule, 'Moorish' dancers were still invited
to perform at the great ceremonies of state. A Muslim ancestry may
perhaps still be detected in the haunting folk music of the Alfama
quarter of Lisbon. The winding Muslim alleys survive today much
as they were when conquered by English crusaders in AD 1147.

The Portuguese wars of religion began long before the European
crusading movement brought seaborne mercenaries heading for the
Holy Land on to the scene. In the mountains of northern Iberia
Christian politics had survived on a small scale almost throughout
the Muslim era. By the eleventh Christian century these northern
people were raiding deep into Muslim territory, beyond Braga in

Portugal and down to Toledo in Spain. At the same time renewed military vigour was coming out of Africa to impose a new dynasty, the Almoravids, over Muslim Iberia. The Christian call for foreign help evoked a response among the tribes of France. The monks of Cluny encouraged French knights with their armed followers to join the religious wars in Portugal. By the end of the eleventh century one Henry from Burgundy dominated the land around the harbour of Oporto on the Douro River known as 'Portugal', the land of the port. On 9 April 1097, thirty-one years after the French Duke of Normandy had conquered England, Henry's Burgundian earldom laid claim to the Atlantic plains of Portugal from the Minho River to the Mondego River. A Christian state was emerging to challenge the walled cities and high castles of the Muslim states in Portugal.

The earldom of Portugal soon aspired to the status of kingdom of Portugal and Henry's son Afonso Henriques established his royal capital in the heavily fortified city of Guimarães, not far from the archiepiscopal see of Braga. His pretensions were severely challenged on two fronts. In the north the Christian kings who later conquered Castile claimed supremacy and Portugal was compelled to invest extensive resources in training and equipping military personnel and in building stone fortifications. In the south Portugal's aspirations to dominate the plains of the Tagus River were challenged by Muslim communities under Almoravid domination. Portugal nevertheless pushed southward in the first half of the twelfth century and moved the capital first to Coimbra and then to Lisbon after crusaders had captured it in a particularly gruesome orgy of blood-letting. In the second half of the twelfth century Muslim power revived under the Almohad dynasty which had crossed over to Europe from Morocco, but in the thirteenth century the advantage turned once again to the Christians. Meanwhile the northern frontier remained deeply embattled causing much stress in Portuguese medieval society. Collaboration between the nobility and the monarchy regularly broke down and the feudal contract was spasmodically replaced with royal authority exercised by ecclesiastical lawyers trained at the university of Bologna in Italy. A mounting challenge to this royal authoritarianism culminated in a Christian civil war in 1245.

The wars of religion in Portugal did much to impoverish the country after the long period of Muslim tranquillity. Not only did war bring with it famine, flight and the spread of disease, it also disrupted the path of economic progress. As the Christian raids bit deeper into the south, sometimes followed by permanent Christian occupation, so Portuguese Muslims sought to emigrate to calmer and more prosperous regions in Spain and Morocco. Sections of the conquered land were partially depopulated and immigrants from the north lived off them wastefully and extensively rather than investing in advanced productive farming. Muslims who stayed behind often found themselves enslaved or at best given a reduced status. The Christian ghettos of the Muslim towns, on the other hand, provided the new local leadership. The most artistic aspect of Christian colonisation was the establishment of Cistercian monasteries on the old Muslim lands. The great abbey of Alcobaça was but one Portuguese representation of flowering medieval architecture. Monastic colonisation and agricultural development contrasted with the more mercenary activities of the Christian military orders, such as the Templars, which also took a leading part in the wars. After AD 1250, however, nation building took on a more constructive form as the two halves of Portugal were brought together.

In 1256 the resuscitated monarchy, adopting French models of incipient democracy, convened a parliament, or 'cortes', to talk out the differences of national ambition. The aspirations of the nobles were partially satisfied in one more round of territorial expansion when the Christians of Portugal conquered the neighbouring Algarve and replenished their fortunes in the old plundering style. The great 'Moorish' castles of the Algarve, Islam's Atlantic 'Kingdom of the West', were awarded to Christian conquerors. In order to avoid a debilitating haemorrhage of productive peoples, however, the new rulers gave some civic and economic rights to their Muslim subjects. Christian toleration of Muslim religious practices was not as complete as Muslim toleration of Christian worship had been but Islam did survive for some centuries among peasants and artisans and the mild land of orchards and fisheries continued to prosper gently as a semi-autonomous kingdom whose ruler also wore the crown of Portugal.

The Christian conquest of the Algarve had the severe disadvantage of bringing Portugal into acute conflict with Castile. This conflict was to dominate the foreign policy of Portugal for the next seven

3 The southern plain of Portugal around Evora was colonised by Romans, who built the now-ruined temple of Diana (centre of photograph), by Muslims who fortified the hilltop city, and by Christians whose kings frequently resided there.

hundred years. The southward expansion of Castile from the high plateau of central Spain had closely paralleled the expansion of Portugal. Portugal, however, had the advantage of constant access to the Atlantic coast. Castile's demand for an outlet to the sea led to claims on the Muslim west which the Portuguese conquest of the Algarve thwarted. Castile was compelled to develop its overseas trade through the conquered river ports of Andalusia, Seville and Córdoba, rather than the ocean ports of Lagos and Tavira to which it aspired. The conflict did not end with the fall of the Algarve, and confrontation between Portugal and its eastern neighbour intensified. The military tradition of maintaining frontier castles to protect the realm was no longer directed at Muslim enemies in the south but at fellow Christians in the east. The frontier fortresses were periodically reinforced right through until the great war of Portuguese independence that began in 1640. The financing of defence imposed a burden on the Portuguese exchequer which further exacerbated the difficult search for a social balance between the rival layers of post-conquest society.

Portuguese society was divided into three very different geographical regions in the centuries following the wars of religion. In the north a feudal hierarchy of contractual relations dominated an essentially agrarian economy. The supply of labour to the barons in return for a share of the crops and a minimal protection against neighbourhood aggressors was the basis of the social contract. The system was exploitative, violent and unstable but it survived even such large-scale fourteenth-century catastrophes as the Black Death and a 'peasants' revolt', both of which affected Portugal in much the same way and at much the same time as they affected England. In central Portugal the focus was on the towns and rather different class affiliations evolved. A 'bourgeoisie' of middle-class burghers gained influence in the burghs and gained their wealth from crafts and commerce. Power resided in the municipalities rather than with the barons. The town demand for food helped enrich the landowners of the central plains but the town demand for labour drained workers off the farms and created a scarcity of fieldhands. In an attempt to retain their vassals, landowners began to award them limited land rights in return for payments in cash or kind. In the south it was neither the northern-style barons nor the plains-style municipalities which dominated society but the knights of the religious orders. Their estates were worked by Christian immigrants and Muslim slaves. Throughout the country labour service was demanded and resisted in a pattern of co-operation and confrontation of varying intensity. In 1373 the city of Lisbon imposed obligatory labour dues of particular severity when the burghers decided that they needed a new city wall to protect themselves from rebellious rustics as well as from alien intruders. Tensions rose and within ten years the countryside was in open rebellion and the monarchy lost control of its kingdom.

The revolution of 1383 laid the foundations of early modern society in Portugal. Not only did the peasants rebel against the barons, but the burghers rebelled against the crown. Rival claimants to the regency of the vacant throne drummed up support in both town and country, opening the way to extensive participation in political affairs. In the confusion the bishop of Lisbon was lynched, and an illegitimate prince led a palace coup and was acclaimed by the mob as the defender of the realm. The prince, John of Avis, was master of the religious military Order of Avis, and was able to obtain support from other military orders when he left the city to recruit nationwide support in a civil war. Castile took the disorders as an opportunity to intervene and besieged Lisbon in a vain endeavour to put its preferred royal faction in power. Plague descended on the city, however, and forced the Spaniards to lift the siege. After two years of upheaval the Portuguese parliament met at Coimbra and declared the throne vacant. The eleven churchmen, seventy-two noblemen and knights of the military orders, and fifty commoners representing the municipalities then elected the Master of Avis to be king of Portugal with the title John I. Castile immediately invaded again only to be defeated by a coalition of Portuguese factions at the great battle of Aljubarrota on 14 August 1385. The victors set to work designing Portugal's finest monastery, Batalha, and Lisbon sponsored the building of a great Carmelite church of thanksgiving. Portugal's elected dynasty had won internal support and international respect in a resounding victory over one of the great powers.

The Avis dynasty began its ascent in international relations by seeking a stable alliance against Castile to serve it in the future. One obvious potential partner was England, that other small Atlantic

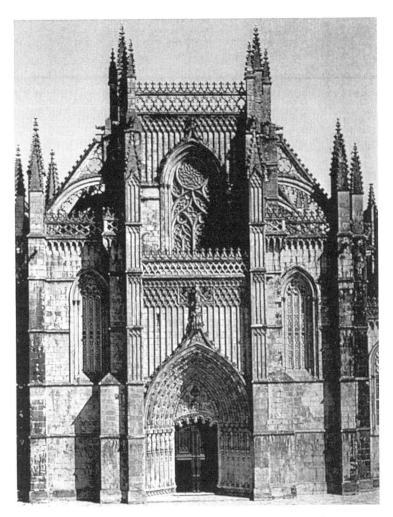

4   The construction of the monastery of Batalha was begun
after the battle of Aljubarrota which confirmed the election of
John I of Avis to the throne, cemented the English alliance and
drove out the Castilian invaders.

kingdom on the western fringe of great power politics. Relations
between Portugal and England had fluctuated ever since an English
crusader had become the first bishop of Lisbon. Later, during the
first decades of the Hundred Years War, Portugal had intermittently

sided with England. Now John I signed a 'perpetual alliance', sealed at Windsor in 1386, which was to be the bedrock of Portuguese diplomacy until well into the twentieth century. He also married Philippa of Lancaster, granddaughter of Edward III of England; their sons, the royal princes, carried Portugal to the edge of the modern age. Edward (Duarte) became king and won the support of the nobility, Peter (Pedro) patronised the towns and encouraged the commercial growth of Lisbon, and Henry (Henrique), the so-called Navigator, became commander of the military Order of Christ and laid the foundations of a worldwide Portuguese empire. The only unexpected twist on the distant horizon concerned John's illegitimate son, Afonso, who married the daughter of his military commander, thus acquiring extensive estates gained during the war with Castile. They founded the nation's wealthiest family of dukes, the Braganzas, and it was they who eventually gained power in 1640, revived the English alliance after eighty years of Castilian captivity, and restored an empire ravaged by forty years of Dutch attack. Before that, however, Portugal had enjoyed its first golden age under the legitimate Anglo-Portuguese branch of the Avis dynasty.

After being subject to two millennia of colonisation by Phoenicians and by Romans, by Muslims and by Christians, the Portuguese embarked on their own career of imperial expansion and settler colonisation. Their first successes were on the islands in the Atlantic. In the Canary Islands they had to enslave the indigenous Berbers before turning the conquerors into landowners with a mandate to grow vines and sell canary wine. The scheme was successful and Tenerife in particular attracted many land-hungry immigrants, but after half a century of Portuguese activity the Canaries were transferred to Castile in one of the many peace treaties that tried to abate intra-Iberian rivalry. A longer-term Portuguese project, also sponsored by Prince Henry and his military order, brought Portuguese settlers to the vacant islands of Madeira and the Azores where wheat was successfully introduced to supplement the internal farm trade of Portugal and to supply corn to Lisbon by ship rather than by ox cart. Yet further afield the colonisation of the Cape Verde Islands led to the development of a textile industry based on slave-grown cotton and indigo dyes. Even deeper into the tropics the West African island of São Tomé was planted with sugar cane harvested by black slaves. Thus in the space of one hundred years Portugal had experimented with colonial models for growing the great crops that were to dominate world trade over many centuries.

The second feature of Portugal's imperial ambition was even more adventurous than its initiation of island colonisation. The Avis dynasty aspired to cross the Strait of Gibraltar and conquer the African mainland. In previous ages Iberia and the Maghreb had commonly been dominated by the same political culture, Roman or Germanic or Arab, and now Christian kings sought to unify Portugal and Morocco. The lure was land which attracted both the nobility of northern Portugal and the southern knights of the military orders. The soils of Portugal were fertile but scarce in the north and plentiful but sterile in the south. North Africa, formerly the breadbasket of Rome, appeared to offer great plains where wheat could be grown in abundance if only the Muslim peasants could be dominated by Christian knights as they had been in the southern plains of Portugal and the Algarve. The Master of Avis and his sons sought to give a third thrust to the *reconquista* following the twelfth-century conquest of central Portugal and the thirteenth-century conquest of the Algarve and thereby enrich their supporters with new African territory and new vassals subdued in approved style. The venture did not prosper but one feat of arms went down in history. That was the capture of the fortified city of Ceuta, taken from the Moroccan resistance in 1415. Prince Henry won his spurs at Ceuta and the event symbolised the end of the inward-looking European middle ages and the beginning of the outward-looking age of expansion.

The European age of expansion, led by Portugal, did not owe its success to the land-hungry barons and knights but to the city-bound burghers of Lisbon and Lagos who prospered under the patronage of Prince Pedro. The second lure of Africa was gold. It was known throughout the Italian banking fraternities of Islam and Christendom that much of the Mediterranean world's gold came from West Africa via the Moroccan camel caravans. Portuguese merchants therefore aspired to capture the desert markets of the northern Sahara and to dominate the European supply of foreign gold in much the way that the Almoravids had done in the eleventh century. Despite numerous heroic military ventures the conquest of Morocco always eluded the Portuguese. Their economic intelligence

5 This oak panel painted in 1445 by Nuno Gonçalves shows
the beatified Prince Ferdinand flanked by his sister Isabel of
Burgundy, and his brother Henry 'the Navigator'.

did, however, improve, and slowly they began to skirt the Saharan seaboard in search of alternative routes of access to the mines. By the 1460s they were buying gold in Senegal and within twenty years they had reached the Gold Coast (modern Ghana) and built a stoutly fortified trading post named Saint George of the Mine. A proportion of the gold which had previously gone overland by camel was diverted. The trade was a royal monopoly, administered by an office on the Lisbon waterfront, and very soon it was supplying Portugal with wealth formerly unheard of amounting to half a ton of gold each year.

The high bourgeoisie of Lisbon and their clients did well out of the colonial expansion and gave their full support to Prince Pedro, the merchants' friend, in the round of upheavals that affected the Portuguese body politic when he became regent on the death of his brother King Duarte. The rival court faction of landowners was less enchanted with the rise of the bourgeoisie and eventually stripped the prince of the regency and in the turmoil he lost his life. There was a long lull in the African trade until the nobility recognised that they too could benefit from the new imperialism if in less glittering ways. One great economic weakness of the estates of southern Portugal was the shortage of labour. The knights who raided Morocco were therefore keen to kidnap women and children or to capture prisoners of war who could be sold into slavery on the latifundia of the plains or the old fruit farms of the Algarve. The merchant seamen of Lagos took up slave catching with enthusiasm. When the explorers reached West Africa they began to buy black slaves, sometimes selling horses in exchange. When trading revived in the 1450s the profit on a Mauritanian slave was estimated at 700 per cent. Black immigration into Portugal grew to such prosperous dimensions that southern landowners were able to survive without new frontiers to conquer. In Evora, the greatest city of the south and the first one to have been conquered by Christians, 10 per cent of the population was black at the height of the slave trade to Europe. The lot of African slaves, whether on the farms or in household service, was not a happy one and they were denied many of the legal rights given to the older generations of white slaves who had been subdued in the wars of conquest. Black women slaves, for instance, were not afforded the protection against sexual exploitation that was given

6   In the fifteenth century, before the colonisation of Brazil, black slaves from Africa were used extensively in Portugal for both field and domestic labour.

to white domestics, and young mestiço girls of mixed race were prized as mistresses though not necessarily as wives. Miscegenation meant that within a dozen generations the 35,000 black Africans who had once lived in Portugal had been blended into the mainstream of a somewhat darkened Portuguese race. Only in Lisbon did a small African ghetto survive and specialise in particular skills such as house painting. The longer-term legacy of the traffic in black slaves was to be felt with the opening of the American colonies in the seventeenth century.

The first great colonising breakthrough, following the exploration of the African coast, occurred in 1492 when a Genoese admiral, formerly in Portuguese service but now in the pay of Castile, crossed the Atlantic and opened new vistas of European empires in the Americas. Columbus' own efforts concentrated on the Caribbean islands, but in 1500 Portuguese sailors discovered the southern mainland of Brazil and made good their claims under a papal dispensation. Charters of conquest not unlike those used in the conquest of the Moorish lands were awarded by the crown to colonial entrepreneurs willing to invest their money and talent in opening up a new continent. The planting skills developed on the African islands were brought across to Latin America and efforts were made to instil a work discipline into the enslaved native American population. When the private ventures failed, the crown took on direct responsibility for economic exploitation and organised the transportation of black slaves from Africa in the manner that had already proved so successful in Europe. In order to increase the supply of black slaves a Portuguese chartered colony was established in Angola and conquistadores were given the right to subdue African chiefs and force them to pay feudal dues in the form of captives for export. The system was so successful that the trade gradually rose over the next century to 10,000 men, women, children and babies a year. They made Brazil into a sad but prosperous colony.

The second breakthrough in the rise of the Portuguese empire occurred in 1498 when a small fleet commanded by Vasco da Gama reached the coast of India having rounded the African Cape of Good Hope and discovered a direct sea lane from Europe to Asia. Thereafter huge sailing carracks brought Indian pepper and cotton, Indonesian perfume and spice, Chinese silk and porcelain, to the royal trading house at Lisbon. It took thirty years for the old oriental trading houses in Venice, in collaboration with the Ottoman empire, to recapture a significant share of the trade that had formerly gone overland. Although the sea route was long, and the wooden ships liable to decay, to shipwreck and to piracy, the profits on a successful round trip to India were astronomic. To guard the route Portugal built a great fortress at Mombasa in East Africa, established a colonial city at Goa in India, built an entrepot at Macau in China and even created a community of Christian converts at Nagasaki in Japan which flourished until overwhelmed by the reviving power of the Japanese state. For 100 years Portugal virtually monopolised the sea route to Asia.

The wealth of Africa was garnered by John II who ascended the throne in 1481. He used it to build up the power of the monarchy against the nobility, much as Prince Pedro had done during his regency one generation before. The confrontation between king and nobles culminated in the execution of Portugal's premier duke, the Duke of Braganza, in a public display of awesome power in the

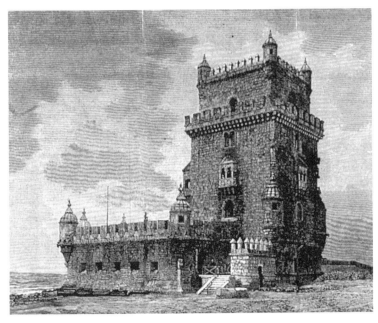

7   The Belem Tower at the mouth of the Lisbon river was built in the ornate 'Manueline' style favoured by King Manuel I in the prosperous years that followed the opening of the seaborne spice trade with India in 1498.

royal city of Evora. Further staged executions split the court into rival factions and isolated the king. He was able to survive by building up a new form of government based on hired clerks who managed new-style administrative departments of state. Eventually the noble interests fought back and when the king died his estranged brother-in-law gained the throne at the head of the noble party in 1495. The new king, Manuel I, continued to use the modern administrative system to govern overseas trade and reigned over a golden age of unforetold imperial prosperity as the wealth of Asia began to pour into Portugal. The Manueline era was particularly noted for its exuberantly ornamented architectural style. The wealth arrived at the seaports of Lisbon and Lagos, but the ostentation was displayed in the royal residences built or refurbished in the provinces. Celebration of the new prosperity also took the form of religious thanksgiving and church patronage of the arts. The triple alliance of the landed nobility, the church aristocracy and the peripatetic court remained powerful despite its dependence on the merchant class of the ports. In order to protect the traditional power of the nobility Manuel adopted new Spanish-style measures to keep the rising bourgeoisie in the subservience from which they had twice broken free during the fifteenth century.

It was perhaps no accident that the opening of the European overseas empires coincided with a fundamental transformation of social relations inside the Iberian peninsula. In 1492, just before Columbus reached America, Castile broke its long-standing pattern of alliances and rivalries with Granada. In a lightning invasion the old Muslim monarchy was overthrown. The coup was politically successful though economically costly. The last Muslim kingdom of western Europe was plundered rather than nurtured by its Christian invaders and many wealthy merchants and silk manufacturers emigrated from Spain. Once Muslim power had been broken, toleration of Muslim religious practices declined sharply and persecution was institutionalised by the Court of Inquisition. The ending of religious toleration in Spain was rapidly emulated in Portugal. In 1497, the very same year that Vasco da Gama set off to open the African route to India, Portugal passed legislation forbidding public worship by either Muslims or Jews. Forced conversions led to the recognition of a new social category of 'New Christians'. Many of the Jewish New Christians were artisans and merchants who played an important economic role in the cities and ports and beyond them in the colonies. They therefore became embroiled in the disputes between the landed nobility which dominated the north and the urban middle class that was so powerful in the central towns of Portugal. The landed interests limited the power of the merchants by accusing them, rightfully and wrongfully, of illegal religious practices. The middle class no longer had a royal patron as it had had under Pedro in the civil war of the 1440s, or during the reign of John II in the 1480s, and so those who opposed the conservative domination at court risked their lives. The nation's need for entrepreneurial skills and the nobility's fear of middle-class power remained in tension for the next three centuries.

The great wealth of King Manuel's Portugal did not long outlast him. Rival routes to India were revived by the Italian city states and

8 This great window in the Convent of Christ, Tomar, repre-
sents one of the most elaborate examples of Portuguese stone
carving in the Manueline style.

9 Sixteenth-century Portuguese seafaring was not only a matter of peaceable exploration and profitable commerce; it often involved armed conflict with enemies afloat and ashore.

the gold fields of West Africa were visited by semi-piratical merchant venturers licensed by Elizabeth of England. The Portuguese nobility turned its attention again to dynastic marriages and in particular to a search for the unification of the Iberian peninsula. In the late 1570s a wild young king, Sebastian, briefly revived the notion of overland conquest as the key to the nation's fortunes and led a military campaign into Morocco. He was defeated and disappeared at the battle of Alcacer Quibir. The royal succession was determined in favour of the Spanish Habsburgs. Philip II of Spain was alleged by the myth-makers to have said of Portugal 'I inherited it, I bought it, and I conquered it', but much of the ruling élite of Portugal in fact felt that their long-term ambition of integration into a multinational, multicultural Iberian empire alongside Andalusia and Aragon had at last been achieved. Nationalist separatism was not a serious issue of high politics though cultural patriotism may have existed at a popular level. The new king meticulously adopted the Portuguese title of Philip I and guaranteed that Portuguese juridical and constitutional autonomy would be secured. For a short while he even moved his chancery from the central Spanish plateau down to Lisbon, his new window on the Atlantic, but *realpolitik* soon required his attention at the heart of the united kingdoms in the newly-founded city of Madrid.

Iberian unification brought opportunity and prosperity to many Portuguese. First and foremost it ended centuries of border conflict which, while it may have benefited soldiers, mercenaries, horse breeders, arms dealers and smugglers, had absorbed too much of the nation's political energy. The Portuguese nobility now gained access to a much wider court culture than the narrow post-feudal high society of their own court. Bishops and aristocrats sought illegitimate preferment in the Castilian domains of Andalusia and even beyond in the Spanish possessions of the Mediterranean. The Portuguese middle class gained even more benefit by illegally but successfully opening up the Spanish American colonies to Portuguese trade. Portuguese emigrants often preferred the silver wealth of Peru to the unhealthy slave colonies of Africa and Brazil. True Castilians complained of the competition and readily accused the Portuguese of being Jewish refugees escaping from the Castilian pogroms. Portuguese commercial acumen, on the other hand, was tacitly welcomed by the Castilian authorities in expanding the wealth of the colonies. By the time Philip II died in 1598 Spanish unification was complete and Spain dominated the world from the West Indies to the East Indies.

2

Rebellion and independence in the seventeenth century

The revolt of the Portuguese began on 1 December 1640. The attack on the union crown of Spain and Portugal came unexpectedly. In the early years of union the crown had been careful not to impose inappropriate burdens on the Portuguese kingdom in order to meet the needs of the Spanish one. By 1640, however, such niceties had been eroded and the military needs of Spain required urgent action. The kingdom of Catalonia, long since joined to the crown of Castile on the far side of Iberia, had rebelled against the Spanish union in June of 1640. Castile immediately demanded that Portuguese conscripts be recruited and marched across the peninsula to put down the Catalan insurrection in the east. The great landowners of the plains of Portugal particularly resented new military levies imposed by the union crown in Madrid. Some refused to mobilise their scarce fieldhands for armed service and to surrender them to Spain for such a campaign. The protesters encouraged their premier duke, John of Braganza, to declare Portuguese independence and so free them permanently from such Castilian impositions. They argued that Spain would not be able to mount repression on two fronts and that a Portuguese rebellion was therefore likely to succeed so long as they struck their blow for freedom while the Catalans were still in revolt. The Braganzas, at their noble seat between Evora city and the Castilian frontier, vacillated. Duke John recognised that should the plot fail he had more lands to lose than any other Portuguese duke. Eventually, however, he agreed to lead the insurrection and to lend the name of his house to an insurgent dynasty. The rebels thereupon invaded the royal palace in Lisbon and expelled the resident representative of the Spanish Habsburgs.

The Braganza insurrection was not, by inception, a popular revolution. Three years earlier, in 1637, a genuinely grass-roots rebellion had been attempted in Portugal. On that occasion it was the peasants who had protested at the level of taxation which the union with Spain imposed upon them. Their cause, however, had not been supported by the landowners who had feared that any popular rebellion might jeopardise their own status and privilege. Indeed it has been argued that the subsequent revolt of the barons in 1640 might have been a pre-emptive strike to prevent another popular uprising when the burden of Spanish unity was becoming even heavier. The Braganza supporters were keenly anxious to avoid turning the world upside down, as was being threatened in England.

The lack of popular initiative in launching the Portuguese independence movement does not mean that there was not a degree of popular enthusiasm for liberation from the Spanish union. Centuries of war with Castile had created deep antagonism between the Portuguese and their only land neighbours. Proverbs warned the people about the dangers of trusting Castilians and ballads emphasised the differences between the two popular cultures. A kind of 'messianic nationalism' grew up in Portugal which recalled the heroic exploits of the lost King Sebastian. The royal messiah was imminently expected to return from Morocco to save the people from their sufferings. Such popular sentiments of Portuguese identity did not greatly affect the higher ranks of society. Court culture was truly transnational up to the time of the revolution. Even Portugal's greatest patriotic poet, Camões, had considered himself Hispanic. The rustic vernacular which became the national language of Portugal was not used in polite society. Castilianisation led Portuguese playwrights to join other artists in seeking patronage in the royal palaces of Madrid rather than in the much smaller noble courts of Portugal.

It was not any sentiment of cultural nationalism in high society which led Portugal towards the revolt of the nobility. It was the economic crisis of the seventeenth century which undermined their acceptance of the Spanish union. The general crisis of Iberia had begun to be felt after 1620 when Spanish affluence was gradually

10   Sebastian, lost in battle in 1578 while trying to invade
Morocco, became a folk hero of Portuguese patriotism after
the restoration of independence in 1640.

curtailed by the decline in colonial silver production. The recession
led to social tensions and some blame fell on the Portuguese. Old
settlers in the silver-mining colony of Peru attributed their *malaise*
to immigrants and expelled Portuguese merchants with racist accusations of Judaism. Hostilities spread to Europe and by the 1630s

community rivalry was rife. The antagonism, further enflamed by the revolt of Catalonia and demands for Portuguese assistance in suppressing it, broke into open revolt in 1640 but the nobility was far from united behind the rebels. About half of Portugal's aristocrats, many of them raised to the peerage under the union crown, remained loyal to Spain. By retaining their faith in the Habsburgs the loyalists expected rewards of land and money, or even governorships in Spain's Mediterranean territories. The Braganza 'rebels' stripped the Habsburg 'loyalists' of their titles and gradually created thirty new peerages for their supporters, doubling the size of the surviving aristocracy. The wealthiest estates clustered around the plains city of Evora where the new dynasty had its roots.

The nobility were not the only reluctant rebels in seventeenth-century Portugal. The urban middle class in the port city of Lisbon was also divided in its attitude to the secessionist regime. It is true that bureaucrats made an early transition to the Braganza cause and government continued initially to function more or less uninterrupted. In the financial and commercial community, on the other hand, many entrepreneurs preferred open frontiers and feared the concept of a nationalism that might erect patriotic boundaries around Portugal. Secession, it was argued, might put Portuguese investments in Seville and the Americas at risk. On the other side of the argument it was countered that secession could open up trade with Spain's former dependencies in The Netherlands and give Portugal better access to the great inland markets of the Rhine basin. The Dutch factor was to prove an important one in Portugal's wars of liberation. Not only had the Dutch become active traders in the Portuguese colonies during the Habsburg era, but The Netherlands had become a political and economic haven for many Portuguese exiles of Jewish descent. They had fled to Amsterdam with their ships and their investments when religious intolerance had become more harsh during the Spanish domination.

The Catholic church, like the nobility and the bourgeoisie, faced an unexpected dilemma when the Portuguese uprising broke out. Village priests and the humbler monks may have raised a rebellious cheer for the Duke of Braganza and identified themselves with autonomous Portuguese folk culture but the great abbots and bishops were well integrated into the Castilianised élite and were reluctant to sever their links with international society fearing that national secession might encourage rather than discourage popular rebellion and so threaten their hierarchical order of privilege. Opposition to the conservative religious view was most fearlessly expressed by some Jesuits priests who thereby gained influence at the new court and even supported quite radical political and economic thinking.

The Jesuits had been founded as an arm of the Counter Reformation in the 1540s and in 1558 the Portuguese chapter had established its own university at Evora as a modernising competitor to the archaic university of Coimbra. Jesuit educators countered conservative accusations of subversiveness and claimed that although they were furthering knowledge they were also holding at bay the forces of humanism and nationalism. Their educational programme used Latin exclusively in order to exclude from Portugal the thriving vernacular literatures that were sweeping through Europe. The Jesuits scrupulously maintained the index of censorship and banned the philosophies of Descartes and Newton from their syllabus, preferring Aquinas' doctrine of obedience to the open-ended questioning of the new scientific age. A balance between tradition and modernity enabled the Jesuits to wield educational and confessional power over each rising generation of the élite though they met resistance from some of the landed nobility who resented the departure of their sons to the modern world of Evora and the financial city of Lisbon. In the sixteenth century the Jesuits had strongly supported the Lisbon policy of imperial expansion in Africa and Brazil and had themselves gained great wealth from their colonial possessions as well as prestige from their mission field in Asia. In the seventeenth century, despite the disapproval of their patron the pope, the Jesuits came to favour the independence movement and to support the royal Braganza pretender. This brought them into lasting confrontation with the Inquisition.

The Portuguese Inquisition had been established on the Spanish model in 1536 as the repressive rather than the educational branch of the Counter Reformation. Its quasi-autonomous power could resist the influence of the crown and was even immune from papal interference. Its officers and informers inspired the same dread fear that the 'secret' police of a later age came to inflict on Portuguese society.

11   The medieval university of Coimbra was the bastion of
Portuguese conservatism, though challenged by the Jesuits of
the sixteenth century, an enlightened despot of the eighteenth
century and the republicans of the twentieth century. Its most
famous graduate was António Salazar, who lectured in financial
law before becoming minister of finance in 1928.

Its cruelty in the treatment of alleged religious suspects was widely publicised as a form of social control and its executions were stage-managed to maximum effect. Under the Habsburgs the Inquisition had become an important if somewhat covert tool of government with authority to act on its own initiative without parliamentary or judicial sanction. It was a powerful weapon for the suppression of dissent and was favoured by the landed aristocracy in preserving an old conservative order. The Inquisition's predilection for crushing all innovation in the name of tradition, of conformity and of racial purity brought it into frequent conflict with all Portuguese modernisers. It was not surprising that in 1640 the Inquisition favoured the preservation of Iberian unity and Spanish order and immediately began to mobilise its supporters to crush the Braganza revolt. In July 1641 the Inquisitor-General gave his support to a conspiratorial counter-revolution mounted by one duke, one marquis, three earls and an archbishop. This grand plot to preserve the Spanish connection failed to dislodge the rebellious Braganza 'king' but it signalled a long war of independence punctuated by frequent internal threats to the political stability of the new regime.

The Spaniards appeared to possess one ideological ace in their attempt to suppress the Braganza revolt and reconquer the lost province of Portugal. This was the unflinching hostility of the papacy to the Portuguese cause. Nationalism was not much favoured by the seventeenth-century Vatican. The popes associated political independence with the Protestant religious autonomy which had swept northern Europe. Even if the pope had been inclined to support Portuguese independence in 1640 he would not have dared to offend Spain, the largest of the surviving Catholic powers. The Portuguese rebel armies were therefore handicapped by a lack of papal approbation or any supreme assurance that God was on their side. Despite this papal ostracism, and the persisting inability of Portugal to replace bishops who died, a quasi-autonomous Catholic church survived throughout the twenty-eight-year war of independence. Many monasteries owned good land and flourished economically, while the nobility gave wartime support to local churches with artistic and other patronage. Village padres continued to wield influence over their often fear-ridden congregations and lay administrators husbanded the resources of vacant bishoprics. Portugal remained a bastion of Catholicism despite its long-running feud with their most Catholic majesties of Spain.

The Portuguese rebels adopted 'restoration' as their political slogan though the reality was somewhat different. The system of government they sought to impose was in fact modelled on the one created by the Habsburgs and not at all on a return to the sixteenth century. Under Spanish domination royal power had been exercised by royal officials and a council of government. John IV hoped to balance and restrict the liberated aspirations of nobles, of commoners and of ecclesiastics by adopting similar institutions to enhance royal authority. His problem, however, was that although the aristocracy was willing to encourage the Braganzas to make a pre-emptive strike against popular revolutionary demands, it was not willing to give the new king a licence to establish an absolute monarchy. Kings in Portugal were to be appointed by parliament and not divinely anointed. Furthermore the new crown became dependent on parliamentary approval for all revenue, even for defence spending against Spain. The peers constantly claimed exemption from taxation and the church refused to waive its historic immunity from state levies. Both pointed to the third estate as the traditional source of government income. The king was too weak to impose taxation that the Habsburgs had failed to raise, and too isolated to override the nobility or the church. The reluctant monarch had to acknowledge that parliament could not only limit his divine right but also force him to subsidise the war of liberation out of the revenues from his private estates.

The new king's survival owed much to the tact and skill of his first chief minister, Francisco de Lucena. Under the Habsburgs Lucena had been secretary of the governing council of Portugal for thirty-six years and was therefore the most experienced administrator in the country. As a good bureaucrat he transferred his services to the new *de facto* power in the royal palace at Lisbon but attempted to avoid any unnecessary offence to Spain where his son continued to serve the Habsburgs and could have been a potential victim of reprisals against Portuguese separatists. To prevent unnecessary structural or social changes the chief minister confirmed office-holders in their posts and created no vacancies with which to reward the rebel supporters of the revolution. He also vetoed the prosecution of any

Spanish loyalists who had 'collaborated' with Madrid. This smooth transition was rudely interrupted, however, when in February 1641 Portuguese popular aspirations boiled over in frustrated expectation. The failed revolution of 1637 was remembered and demands for social justice were proclaimed. The nobility took fright and spoke of the 'Lisbon Terror'. Spain probably encouraged the panic of the propertied class and warned that proper order could only be restored if the Braganza 'usurper' were dethroned. The chief minister acted with great firmness to quell an aristocratic counter-revolution and the high-born ring-leaders were ostentatiously executed to defend the Braganza throne.

The power which the crown gained from the execution of the counter-revolutionaries of 1641 troubled a nobility anxious to preserve its own influence and to impose restraints on central government. In the absence of any alternative candidate for the throne, and given the implausibility of contemplating a republican solution of the Dutch type, the aristocratic enemies of royal absolutism struck out at the king's officials. The chief minister who had served them so well in the first months of independence, and whom they had tolerated in high office because he was a mere commoner expected to bend to their will, had proved himself to be sufficiently powerful to execute noble opponents. Lucena's strength in loyalty to his king resembled that of France's chief minister, Richelieu, and his might threatened the influence of the aristocracy. Lucena was arraigned on a charge of treason and condemned without the king being able to save him. He was publicly beheaded in Evora city square by an executioner who symbolically used the same sword that had been used against the king's enemies. In the continuing struggle between crown and parliament a much weaker chief minister was imposed on the king. With such powerful aristocrats restricting his room for political manoeuvre King John looked abroad for support.

The Portuguese revolt of 1640 cannot be interpreted simply as a domestic struggle for power in one corner of the Iberian peninsula which rather unexpectedly resulted in the emergence of an independent state. The revolution occurred in the middle of one of the greatest transformations which Europe had experienced. The Thirty Years War, the rise of modern France and the English Revolution all had a direct bearing on the protracted Portuguese attempt to break away from Spain. The general crisis of early modern Europe affected international trade, in which Portugal still had a colonial role to play. It affected ideology and the great scientific challenge to the papal monopoly of learning of which Portugal was a victim. The crisis also concerned diplomacy and Portugal became the pawn of several conflicting strategies. All these strands were woven together in a generalised European confrontation between north and south. During the conflict Portugal, which was ideologically one of the most conservative countries of the Catholic south, became a captive economic enclave of the Protestant north.

At first the European powers took little notice of yet another Spanish provincial rebellion. Had they done so the matter would have been overshadowed by the simultaneous rebellion of the more powerful and prosperous Catalonia or by the southern revolt of Andalusia which was led in 1641 by one of John of Braganza's relatives by marriage. The international neglect of Portuguese affairs occurred when the great nations of France, England and The Netherlands were all fighting civil, religious or international wars of their own to establish their status and identity in the early modern world. Portugal's international importance as the European link with India had been significantly eroded by the rise of the great Dutch trading corporations of the early seventeenth century. Although Protestant statesmen were not greatly concerned by the papal ban on diplomatic relations with the Portuguese rebels, they were slow to foresee that the rebellion might be successful and that recognition of an independent Portugal might be to their advantage. When recognition did come the initiative was taken by England, the maritime rival to The Netherlands and Portugal's erstwhile medieval ally in north-south European co-operation. The future of Portugal's Asian empire was one of the issues at stake.

By 1640 the Portuguese pepper empire in Asia had entered its twilight years. Despite this economic decline India featured as a romantic colossus in the Portuguese popular imagination. The empire of the east still contained fifty-odd beach-heads, fortresses, trading factories and islands stretching from the Zambezi to the Pacific. The viceroy loosely oversaw the web of merchandising from his island-city of Goa. To the north of the city lay the main centres of Indian textile weaving and dyeing. To the south Goa dominated the pepper plantations of Malabar. Imperial exaggeration claimed that Goa rivalled London or Antwerp at the dawn of the seventeenth century with nearly a quarter of a million inhabitants. The majority of the population were slaves, and colonial households commonly had a dozen guards, stewards and housemaids supporting their masters in almost Roman opulence. Slave artisans and craftsmen were recruited in Mozambique while free Hindu immigrants set up shop as tinkers and goldsmiths, barbers and grocers. The foreign community came from as far away as Armenia and Malaysia but the colonial 'aristocracy' was European. Eurasian children did not qualify for the same status as kingdom-born whites from the mother country, but in times of crisis they were recruited to swell the army's ranks along with black slaves and Christianised Indians.

On completion of their bachelor services immigrant soldier-settlers from Portugal could contract formal marriages and become citizen-settlers. Some of them married white orphan girls sent to the East for want of a dowry, but most married Asians or Eurasians. In 1640 Goa probably had fewer than one thousand married citizens with full rights to elect the city council and to supervise the finances of the religious charities. At the time Goa may have had more monks than voting citizens, but the church, like the state, maintained rigorous conventions about race, and promotion through the ecclesiastical hierarchy had more to do with skin colour than education or culture. In order to protect their daughters from unsuitable marriages to coarse colonial immigrants, or worse, wealthy families endowed comfortable nunneries where white women could live unmolested and free from constant childbearing. The city fathers, however, tried to limit the number of convent places to ensure that they, at least, might find white brides. Both state and church rejoiced in the pomp and splendour of city ceremonial at the hub of the empire.

The threat to this wealthy Indian world in which everyone, priest and soldier, clerk and officer, invested in cinnamon and pepper took many forms. As trading receipts declined defence was neglected, pirates became more daring, and Indian princes more assertive. A truce with the Dutch expired in 1621 and the viceroy, encouraged by Jesuit diplomats, negotiated a local peace treaty with the English in 1635. An English ship was sent to Portuguese China to fetch cannons for

the defence of Goa against the Dutch. The clergy assured the scepti-
cal faithful that the English would concentrate on the pepper trade
and not attempt to disseminate heretical beliefs. This breakthrough
in Catholic–Protestant co-operation did little to stem the rising tide
of Dutch economic power in Asia, but it did present a diplomatic
model for Anglo-Portuguese treaties in Europe in 1642 and 1654.
Asia, however, did not otherwise play as significant a part in the
war of independence as did the Atlantic colonies where the cold
war between Calvinist Europe and Catholic Europe generated fierce
battles.

Portugal's Atlantic empire had fared as badly as the Asian empire
during the 'Spanish captivity'. The Dutch, who gained their independence from Spain in the 1580s, exactly as the Portuguese were
losing theirs, penetrated the Atlantic empire at several points during a long struggle for hegemony. Already by 1605 the Dutch were
the great carriers of the South Atlantic and in that year 180 Dutch
ships visited the salt pans of South America. By 1621 they dominated sugar freight as well, building a dozen new vessels a year for
the Brazil trade and keeping twenty-nine sugar refineries in business
with 40,000 chests of raw sugar. More than half of Portugal's colonial traffic was carried in Dutch bottoms almost regardless of the
state of political and diplomatic relations. The Portuguese shipping
agents were frequently members of Lisbon's class of New Christian
merchants whose Jewish families had been forcibly converted in
past generations. They often had good connections with the Jewish
community in Amsterdam, many of whom were themselves exiles
from Portugal. The Luso-Dutch trade was sufficiently vibrant to
attract large-scale French and Venetian investment across national
and ideological boundaries.

Commercial collaboration and rivalry were not the only feature
of Luso-Dutch relations, however, and active war occurred in the
Atlantic theatre as well. In 1630 the Dutch succeeded, at the second
attempt, in conquering the sugar plantations of north-east Brazil
and held them for over twenty years. In 1641 they also captured the
most extensive Portuguese slaving grounds in Africa and held the
Angolan port of Luanda for seven years. Two permanent inroads
also occurred, one in West Africa, where the gold-trading fortress
of Elmina was taken by the Dutch in 1637, and one in South Africa

where The Netherlands fortified the Cape of Good Hope in 1652. Both colonies eventually became British territories.

While the struggle for control of the Atlantic progressed a parallel set of diplomatic initiatives took place in Europe to try to gain recognition for the self-styled king of Portugal. Eventually the Braganzas settled for an alliance with Protestant England, but before doing so they tried long and hard to obtain an alliance with the much stronger and more Catholic king of France. France straddled the north-south divide and had a half-tolerated Protestant minority strongly associated with economic innovation. In the Thirty Years War France increased its northern influence until peace was signed with the German states in 1648. In the south war continued until peace was finally achieved in Spain in 1659. Such a rise in power, and an ability to establish a national identity without severing links with Catholicism, made France the obvious first choice as a midwife to the new Portugal. The French cause, however, did not prosper in Portugal. France welcomed a Portuguese rebellion which weakened Spain and enhanced the prospect of French frontier encroachment on Catalonia, but Portuguese overtures remained of minor importance to French diplomacy. The ambitious Portuguese hope of capturing the wedding of the century by marrying Catherine of Braganza to the young King Louis XIV of France came to nothing. Louis did not marry into a breakaway dynasty of dubious legitimacy which had been deprived of church recognition but held out successfully for the grand Catholic marriage alliance with Spain itself. To protect its minor options, however, France did find a royal princess as consort for John of Braganza's son and discreetly supported Portuguese autonomy as a check on Spanish power. A French party grew up at the Portuguese court and later played a significant role in the military and political denouement of the Portuguese bid for independence. In the meantime, however, England made its presence felt once again in Portuguese affairs.

Diplomatic relations between Portugal and England went through complex contortions during the war of independence. The 'old alliance', which had linked the two nations before the Spanish captivity, had provided England with a supply of wine, a market for woollen cloth, safe havens on the sea roads out of Europe, and an ally against its old enemy and imperial rival, Castile. The prospect of a restored alliance attracted England and negotiations over recognition for the rebel dynasty began in the reign of the absolutist Charles I. Before they could bear fruit, however, England broke into civil war and Portugal quixotically supported the royalist cause. When Charles fell the Braganzas turned in ironic desperation to the regicide Cromwell for help in consolidating their throne. In a treaty signed at Westminster King John agreed to prevent the molesting of the traders of the English 'Lord Protector' and allowed the said traders to use Bibles. With astounding boldness the king also allowed the Protestants to bury their dead on Catholic soil. In 1661, after the restoration of Charles II to the English throne, this treaty was revised at Whitehall on the orders of John's widow, the queen regent of Portugal. It now contained serious military provisions which were eventually to help bring the war of independence to an end. Portugal was allowed to recruit 2,500 soldiers and horses in England at the going market rate for mercenaries hired to fight against Spain. Even more expensively Portugal was allowed to seek out 4,000 fighting men in each of the Celtic dominions of Scotland and Ireland and to charter twenty-four English ships to carry them. The expeditionary force was to be issued with English weapons on arrival and to be guaranteed religious freedom of worship. Further English cavalry and infantry were recruited in the following year. The alliance was then sealed by the marriage of Catherine of Braganza to Charles Stuart of England and Scotland. The princess took with her a huge dowry of 2 million pieces of gold and England was offered colonial toe-holds in the Portuguese empire at the African port of Tangier and at the Indian port of Bombay. Servicing the wedding debt burdened the Portuguese exchequer for half a century. The expense was still not enough to guarantee the independence of Portugal, but further help was to hand from a wholly unexpected quarter. This was Portugal's own Latin American empire in Brazil.

The Braganza family was firmly rooted in the agriculture of the great plain of Portugal and knew little of colonial affairs. It therefore came as a surprise to John IV to discover that Brazil was to play a central diplomatic role during his reign. It was the Jesuit lobby that took the lead in persuading the rebel king that the Latin American colonies could be used to ensure the success of his revolution. The Jesuits had gained great influence in Latin America by building up

European-owned estates in which converts could live in Christian communities. Moreover mission priests had formed an alliance of convenience with normally hostile and jealous secular colonists who shared their anxiety over the religious, economic and political threat presented by the Dutch in northern Brazil. When news of the Braganza revolt in Europe reached Brazil, the leading citizen of Rio de Janeiro, Salvador de Sá, made common cause with the Jesuits and agreed to support Portuguese independence.

Part of Salvador de Sá's motivation in backing the Jesuits and allying himself with the Braganzas related to losses in Africa. The Luso-Dutch war in Angola was one of the remotest theatres of the Thirty Years War. The Dutch had originally tried to capture the port of Luanda in 1624 and only vigorous attention to the colonial defences by a noble Portuguese governor appointed by the Habsburgs prevented Dutch success in seizing the source of South America's annual supply of 10,000 Angolan slaves. In 1641 the Dutch renewed the attack, anxious to capture the colony before peace negotiations resulted in the recognition of the breakaway Portuguese dynasty. The Portuguese garrison in Angola fled up-river and in a remote African exile tried to decide whether to accept Dutch sovereignty, whether to remain loyal to the Habsburgs or whether to raise the standard of rebellion on behalf of the Braganzas. They chose the Braganzas and appealed to Rio de Janeiro for help in fending off both African and Dutch attacks on their fortified municipal enclave. It was seven years before they were finally rescued when Salvador de Sá arrived in Africa and the Brazilians expelled the Dutch from Luanda in 1648. The place was handed unexpectedly to King John who was mildly embarrassed by this local breach of the peace he had secured with the Dutch. The reconquest of colonies previously taken by the Dutch did not end there, however, and six years later the Brazilians recovered the great plantation colonies of north-east Brazil, driving the Dutch to concentrate instead on their trade with the Caribbean. Portugal's bid for independence was thus supported by the South American colonies and their African dependencies.

In 1656 King John IV of Portugal died. Although he had regained control of his South Atlantic empire in Brazil and Angola, he had not gained recognition of his unilateral declaration of independence in Europe. During his reign parliament had met three times to legitimate the dynasty and raise revenue for the war but without complete success. When John's powerful Spanish widow took over the regency of the rebellious kingdom she had to continue the search for an accommodation with Spain but the war dragged on. At home the aristocracy took advantage of the king's death further to increase its domestic influence and limit the power of the royal administration. In 1659, however, the affairs of Portugal began to change rapidly. The Treaty of the Pyrenees ended Spain's long war with France and altered the international scene. Far from bringing diplomatic gains to Portugal the peace freed Spanish troops to attempt once more the suppression of the rumbling Portuguese rebellion. The renewed Spanish invasions led by Philip IV's son failed, however, to achieve the reconquest of the breakaway kingdom. On the contrary, the last phase of the war brought victory to the Portuguese thanks to large-scale mercenary assistance from the outside world.

The successful phase of the war of liberation began in 1662 with a *coup d'état* in the royal palace in Lisbon. The expensive marriage of Catherine of Braganza to the Protestant English king had been neither popular nor politic and brought bitter criticism of the regency. Renewed attack from Spain heightened popular tension and caused serious panic in Lisbon with the looting of aristocratic properties. A restive younger faction of the nobility overthrew the queen regent and installed the twenty-six-year-old Count of Castelo Melhor as a wartime 'dictator' supported by the queen's wild and possibly retarded son who became nominal king. The new regime decided radically to alter Portugal's pattern of international relations and switch from the English alliance to a French one. The adolescent king was married to a French princess and the young dictator modelled his government on the royal absolutism of the Bourbon dynasty with its cardinal-ministers. Opposition to the pro-French dictatorship by the new king's younger brother, Prince Pedro, and by his sister, Queen Catherine of England, was swept aside. Castelo Melhor's military prowess, and the recruitment of international mercenaries under the brilliant command of the Franco-German Marshal Schomberg, led to three years of vigorous war against the tired troops of Spain. After several decisive battles Portuguese victory was secured in 1665. Two years later the French party and its dictator were overthrown in another palace *putsch*. Prince Pedro and the English party seized power, and in 1668 Spain finally recognised the 'legitimacy' of the Braganza dynasty and the Peace of Westminster was ratified. Pedro, although only titled Prince Regent for the first half of his 'reign', brought forty years of political continuity to the court of Portugal.

Prince Pedro's usurpation of his brother's throne brought fundamental changes to the politics of Portugal. The inept young king was bundled off to exile in the Azores Islands in the mid-Atlantic. The young dictator with the absolutist aspirations fled the country, ironically to seek asylum in England. Portugal rejected the French alliance, though Pedro shored up his political position by marrying his deposed brother's estranged French wife. All the territories which Spain had occupied during the final campaign for independence were restored to Portugal with the single exception of the Moroccan fortress-city of Ceuta dominating the Strait of Gibraltar. The absolutist tendencies seen under the dictatorship were curtailed and the old nobility temporarily recovered some of its influence. Government was again in the hands of an oligarchy of courtiers rather than under the control of royally appointed officers. The old alliance with England was restored and Lisbon became an enclave of northern mercantilism, a miniature London, thronged with new trading ships built at Amsterdam. All round the Lisbon enclave rural Portugal was a sea of agrarian Catholicism where provincial nobles commissioned chapels in the Italian style and the gentry built their manor houses with an eye on French concepts of grandeur.

The peace of 1668 should have left Portugal free from the drain of defence expenditure and ready to make the great leap forward to escape from its impoverishment. Prosperity, however, continued to be elusive. The nearest thing that Portugal had to a domestic industry of international importance was the salt industry. Salt had been a vital economic asset during the war and the Dutch market had been extended to the Baltic as well. In the 1660s salt prices in Amsterdam were high and facilitated Portugal's final achievement of independence. Since the Portuguese merchant fleet was never large enough to carry salt to the customers, hundreds of small boats came south every season to buy 80,000 tons of salt on the Portuguese beaches. Portugal's ability to pay for its imports with salt benefited the salt

12   Detail of an engraving depicting the Lisbon waterfront,
c. 1620, showing the west wing and dock of the royal palace.

industry, though with rather low levels of added value, but damp-
ened the development of domestic manufacturing crafts. Lisbon
society could buy its textiles, clothing, household appliances, metal
wares, porcelain, ornaments and luxuries abroad on the salt budget without the need to foster domestic artisanship or increase rural
productivity. The pitfall of under-development, of selling raw and

13   An early eighteenth-century tiled mural depicting the figure of death, in the cloister of São Vicente de Fora, Lisbon.

buying processed, plagued the economy of restoration Portugal from
the start.

Portugal's second great shore-line industry, fishing, also failed to
bring the anticipated prosperity. Fish was a more important part of
diet than meat for coastal peoples and port-dwellers but the growth
of the overseas colonies had denuded the industry of maritime skills
as fishermen were commandeered to serve on the great sea lanes
of the empire. Fishermen also suffered from a shortage of fishing
vessels as boats were taken for long-distance commerce, shipbuilders
had other priorities of naval construction and ships' timbers had
to be expensively imported from Sweden and Brazil rather than
hauled by ox cart from the inland forests of Portugal. Portugal's
economic dependence became acute when the fishing industry was
so starved of capital that even the national staple of dried codfish
could no longer be supplied by the home industry. The country
which had pioneered the exploitation of the great fishing banks of
Labrador and Newfoundland, came to depend on English fleets for

its North Atlantic cod. Even more dramatically Portugal allowed English fishermen to sell dried cod from the British North American colonies direct to the plantation markets of Brazil. This opening was in flagrant breach of conventional mercantilism which insisted that all trade must pass through the metropolis and enhance the wealth of the mother country.

The Lisbon food supply faced an even greater and older crisis than the shortage of codfish. This was the lack of adequate corn marketing facilities. It seemed easier and more profitable to buy grain on the international market than to invest scarce capital and labour in the management and transport needed to improve domestic farming. The Portuguese cereal crisis had affected the city since the middle ages and had been one of the incentives for the first colonial expansion. The problem remained as acute as ever in the seventeenth century. Maize growing only began to alleviate the shortage in the eighteenth century and the corn staples were wheat, rye and barley. Some of the wheat grown on the southern plains could be fetched out by coastal boats sailing up the partially navigable Sado River. The offshore islands, however, remained more accessible when ocean shipping was available. In 1631, before the revolution, Lisbon had imported sixty shiploads of Azores grain in French vessels and a similar quantity of Spanish grain from Seville. After the secession from Spain England became the main supplier of foreign grain and when English surplus supplies were insufficient Lisbon began to buy grain from the English colonies in North America. Portugal thus maintained a tradition of encouraging commerce rather than home agricultural production. The policy of importing 'cheap' food rather than fostering national self-reliance did not, however, improve relations between the urban middle class and the landowning aristocracy.

Since the traditional production of salt, fish and corn was unable to rescue Portugal from its impoverishment the regency government of Prince Pedro sought advice on how to transform the national economy. Three options were presented to free the country from poverty and all three of them were periodically resorted to over the next three centuries. The first and most difficult option was industrialisation. This policy aimed to make more effective use of the country's material resources and human skills. The second option was to export peoples and skills to the empire as migrants and to live off the remittances in cash and kind which they sent home to the mother country. The third option was to export raw materials and primary produce to England and elsewhere and rely on foreign skills for the supply of finished commodities. During his forty-year reign Prince Pedro attempted all three options, beginning with industrialisation.

The basis of a manufacturing policy during the early years of independence was the attempted production of textiles. Portugal's largest single import commodity, and the one which put the greatest strain on the balance of payments, was woven cloth. Although Portugal was a great sheep-rearing nation it exported the bulk of its wool production as a raw commodity for the textile businesses of northern Europe. The prince regent's economic adviser, the Count of Ericeira, therefore recommended that a domestic woollen textile industry modelled on Flemish lines be established in Portugal. 'Factories' were established at Covilhã, nestling at the foot of the central mountain range with easy access to both flocks of sheep and clean mountain water. The experiment, however, like new industrial projects in other developing countries, did not prosper. Economic innovation brought strong antagonism from the traditional weaving guilds of Portugal. They not only feared the competition of better capitalised factory textiles in the market, but anticipated that state enterprises would poach their skilled labour. Commercial middlemen, who made viable profits from farming out piece work to cottage weavers, also protested at the competition. On the other side of the market consumers complained that the local products did not match the quality of English worsteds. Town buyers, with a strong but conservative fashion sense, refused to accept the new national cloth. The government exacerbated the antagonism by protecting the infant industry and imposing limits on the importation of textiles in an effort to save foreign currency. Economic decrees went even further and passed sumptuary laws designed to limit the conspicuous consumption of foreign stuffs by the wealthy élites. The outrage of the import consumers of the city and of the traditional weavers of the countryside was matched by the protest of the provincial nobility which saw industrialisation as a threat to its archaic social order.

The landowning opponents of industrialisation found ideal champions, as might have been expected, in the entrenched defender of traditional values, the Inquisition. During the independence struggle the Inquisition had failed to prevent Portuguese secession from Spain, and under the dictatorship of Castelo Melhor it had campaigned in vain against the French connection and the modernising ideas of economic planning borrowed from Colbert in France. Under the regency of Prince Pedro the inquisitors encouraged the fears of the aristocracy who claimed that industrialisation might give the crown an independent source of income. Such royal freedom, they claimed, would weaken traditional constraints on the crown and facilitate progress towards the type of royal absolutism that they had so strongly opposed both in 1641 and 1662. The Inquisition found no difficulty in obstructing Pedro's industrial policy. Textile manufacturers were accused of being the agents of Jewish capital and were tortured in inquisitional dungeons to frighten off prospective investors. The long incarceration of weavers during judicial investigations of Judaism disrupted production. Convictions led to the confiscation of wealth by jealous accusers, and to achieve the most extreme deterrence some industrialists were publicly executed. This persecution was no simple explosion of aberrant racism and religious bigotry but was a central part of the Portuguese power struggle between modernisers and conservatives.

Religious and racial persecution embittered social and economic divisions in seventeenth-century Portugal much as they were to do in developing countries of later centuries when irrational paranoia gave a keen edge to rational conflicts of interest. The conflict in Portugal was not only a rivalry between town and country, between industrialists and aristocrats, but also a rivalry within the social classes. Portugal had a particularly vigorous 'comprador bourgeoisie' which earned its wealth and status from the import and export businesses. This merchant segment of the middle class had a vested interest in maintaining high levels of international trade rather than in fostering national production and self-sufficiency. Far from being economic nationalists the city wholesalers found themselves bound in a symbiotic relationship with foreign suppliers. Thus it was that the French and their local agents had no desire to see Portugal develop an indigenous silk industry which would limit the Portuguese market for

14   The *haute bourgeoisie* of the English community in Portugal were invited to dine and dance in the great 'Factory House' of the British port merchants of Oporto, in whose 'dessert room' connoisseurs tested their palates.

French silks. The French merchants hindered attempts by Pedro's government to recruit artisans in France and rejoiced over the difficulties which the great drought of 1692 brought to Portuguese silk producers. Importers on the Lisbon waterfront thus found themselves caught up in an unholy alliance of foreign suppliers and noble conservatives both opposed to the government's policy of economic development. The most influential associates of this sector of the bourgeoisie were the English.

The English trading community in Lisbon, known collectively as the 'Factory', was a close-knit and politically privileged community of trade factors with a secure base on the waterfront. Despite the sometimes hysterical xenophobia directed at the English by the Inquisition, members of the Factory retained the right they had won during the war of independence to practise their Protestant worship and maintain their own discreetly walled graveyard. The strategic element which protected the English connection was the royal navy which was more effective than the war fleets of either France or Spain in defending Portugal and its empire from enemy attack. Diplomatically Portugal was also tied to England by Catherine of Braganza who remained queen in Whitehall until 1685. More significant, however, than this strategic and diplomatic tie was the old coalition of Portuguese economic interests which sought to avoid the creation of import-substitution industries and to maintain the English commercial connection. The local agents and retailers associated with the English Factory were naturally content to continue earning a percentage on the supply of English fish, worsted and more particularly wheat. Thus it was that the 'Portugal trade' helped to fuel an agrarian revolution among English corn growers but Portugal did not follow the same path. Instead it turned again to the colonial empire to solve the accruing balance of payments deficit without disturbing the precarious social order which was so resistant to economic innovation.

The old sea empire of Asia had attracted immigrants from the harbours of Portugal and the Algarve to the East in significant but not overwhelming numbers. The restored land empire of the Brazils needed more people to open up the agricultural potential of an underpopulated half-continent. Emigration, especially from the heavily peopled north of Portugal, could be encouraged as an alternative to a domestic agricultural revolution that might radically alter the structures of society, as had been powerfully demonstrated by the experiences of England or France. Portuguese emigration, as an alternative to economic development, did not reach its peak until the nineteenth and twentieth centuries, but it did already occur in the seventeenth century. Migrant sugar and tobacco planters in Brazil were expected to respond to the changing world markets in such ways as to earn Portugal the income to pay for its English imports.

In the later seventeenth century Portugal's growing dependence on Brazilian agriculture became vulnerable to changes in market conditions. In particular the large-scale colonisation of the Caribbean islands by the northern powers led to fierce colonial competition and a decline in sugar prices. To make up for lost revenue and minimise the resulting balance of payments crisis the old Brazilian sugar colony of Bahia diversified into an extension of tobacco production.

A royal tobacco monopoly was established with the distinct advantage to the government that tobacco taxes were awarded not to a trading company but directly to the crown. Colonial tobacco duty became a primary source of royal revenue and avoided much of the old fiscal confrontation between crown and nobility. Brazilian export tobacco was prepared in two-and-a-half-hundredweight rolls coated with molasses and wrapped in cow hides thus giving it excellent qualities of preservation and allowing it to be accumulated for investment and speculation. Portugal sold chewing tobacco to the French and snuff tobacco to Indians. Tobacco also became an important item in the 'assortment' of goods that had to be assembled in Africa in order to buy slaves. Many of the 20,000 rolls of tobacco that the Brazil fleet brought to Europe each year were sold in England, though English planters in Virginia began to build up serious competition. By the 1680s, however, the tobacco trade, like the sugar trade before it, was in recession. In 1688 Portugal was forced to give a price advantage to its re-exports of colonial tobacco by devaluing the Portuguese currency. Ten years later the tobacco planters received a quite different stimulus when the Brazilian gold-rush began and the diggers became large consumers of tobacco.

Neither sugar nor tobacco planters used European immigrants extensively as fieldhands. For the heaviest work they depended on a ready supply of slave labour and seventeenth-century Portugal gained some profit from the buying, feeding, transporting and marketing of some half a million African slave workers. Despite its shortage of ships and mariners Portugal succeeded in managing the great transatlantic migration of captive orphans, prisoners, convicts, debtors, press-ganged labourers and kidnapped travellers who made up the slave trade. In exchange for these human 'commodities', and for a little ivory for the royal monopoly, the slavers supplied West African merchant princes with wine and cloth as well as tobacco. In Angola Brazilian military governors from Rio de Janeiro extended the slaving grounds by armed action, conducting raids 100 miles into the interior to the detriment of the trading communities, both black and white, but to the great profit of the soldiers. The old African kingdoms of Kongo and Angola were effectively destroyed by the colonial wars which followed Portugal's accession to independence but the trade in slaves flourished for the next 200 years.

Colonial wealth, however, was not enough to rescue Portugal from
its seventeenth-century poverty and Prince Pedro's government had
to turn again to the much more controversial question of economic
reform and development on the home front.

  The long-term solution, or half-solution, to the problem of Portugal's agrarian underdevelopment was sought in the wine trade.
The wine trade had a number of advantages as a prospective means
of Portugal's economic salvation. The most simple technical advantage was that raising state revenue from customs dues on export
wines was a simple procedure which did not require any reform
of the rudimentary system of accountancy used by the royal secretaries. To have switched the exchequer's revenue to duties on internal production would have required a bureaucratic revolution that
was probably beyond the means of Portugal's modest educational
system. In addition to the mundane practical advantage of concen-
trating on wine, the wine trade also had the ideological advantage
of not greatly offending the Inquisition and the forces of agrarian
conservatism. It is true that in 1683 Pedro was unable to prevent the
expulsion of the chaplain to the English wine merchants at Oporto
when his heretical behaviour became too blatant, but on the whole
foreign wine merchants were acceptable to the great landowners
who grew vines and produced wine in the old style. The wine shippers sometimes had difficulty in finding assured markets in England
where consumers much preferred claret from Bordeaux to the rather
rough red wines of seventeenth-century Portugal, but endemic war
meant that French wines were not always available. English exporters would have much preferred payment for their cloth to be in
bullion, but when coin was in short supply they accepted payments
in wine. In the early 1680s the Portuguese economy underwent a
modest wine-based revival after the recession of the 1670s. The lead
was given by the island of Madeira.

  Madeira, after its initial colonisation as a wheat island linked
to Portugal by Genoese merchant bankers from Italy, had later
switched its production to sugar until its trade was ruined by the rise
of the great Caribbean sugar plantations with their better soils and
cheaper slave labour. Madeira switched its agrarian strategy again,
this time to wine which it sold to its erstwhile sugar competitors
in the Caribbean. Slowly Madeira wines improved in stability and
quality and a privileged colony of English wine merchants grew up

on the island and began shipping wine to England itself as well as to the English colonies. By the late seventeenth century another focus on English wine exporters had developed on the north mainland of Portugal at Viana and Oporto. An English Factory was established with similar privileges to those of Lisbon and exports rose to 1,000 pipes of wine a year. In the eighteenth century the wine trade from Oporto became one of the great industries of Portugal. Before that, however, other strategies were sought to broaden the base of the country's wealth.

Two political thinkers tried to change the structure of the Portuguese economy in the second half of the seventeenth century, Father António Vieira and the Count of Ericeira. Vieira, a Jesuit writer and close adviser of John IV, had been one of the central figures of the peace negotiations between the Calvinist Dutch and the Catholic Portuguese. He hoped that with independence Portugal would be able to make its peace with the Jewish community and arrange for the repatriation of Portuguese capital which had fled to Amsterdam. He travelled daringly to The Netherlands, causing much scandal by wearing noble rather than ecclesiastical dress, and met the exiles in the Amsterdam synagogue. There he listened to demands for the ending of judicial disabilities imposed on New Christians. The refugees asked that trials for heresy should no longer be based on secret denunciations and on racial presumptions of disloyalty but on specific accusations of illicit worship signed by named accusers. They also asked that any monies returned to Portugal for investment be exempt from judicial confiscation in the event of ecclesiastical persecution. Vieira's attempt to gain a more open religious climate for converted Jews, comparable to that eventually achieved by English Protestants, had only limited success. In the sphere of economic innovation even his own Jesuit order doubted the wisdom of trying to set up Dutch-style joint-stock companies in Portugal since these might restrict Jesuit production in the colonies. The Inquisition was even more radically opposed to Vieira's policy of innovation and toleration. With the support of the landowning nobility it succeeded in getting him confined to the silence of a monastery and subsequently exiled to Rome where he became one of Europe's greatest seventeenth-century preachers but where he lost all political influence over Portuguese affairs. His final departure in 1667 assisted the conservative ascendancy. His initiatives, however, were later revived, albeit abortively, by another economic moderniser and royal adviser, the Count of Ericeira.

It was Ericeira who finally recognised that the forces of social conservatism in Portugal were too strong to allow the government to persist with a policy of industrialisation and that he therefore needed to devalue the currency in order to make traditional agricultural exports competitive with those of rival exporters in the Mediterranean. Although wine producers were the first to benefit from devaluation in 1688, the trade in cork, lemons and wool also felt the fiscal stimulus. Soon afterwards Lisbon exported 10,000 pipes of olive oil as world trade improved. Holland bought 3 million bushels of salt in exchange for Baltic timber, wheat and fish. The English trade in fresh oranges brought in 50,000 gold pieces per year. The transit trade from Brazil to the north European markets benefited from devaluation as well, and 100,000 tanned cowhides a year came from Bahia for the leather and shoe industries. All of this growth, however, was not enough. Exports to England amounting to a quarter of a million pounds sterling did not remotely cover the half million pounds worth of imports. Textile imports alone were worth more than the entire Portuguese export of agricultural produce. The corn deficit still amounted to a million bushels a year. In 1690 Ericeira committed suicide even before the great drought compounded his woes.

The turn of the century saw many changes in Portugal. Prince Pedro, now King Pedro II, had learnt how to balance the factions in his country and had ceased to struggle against conservative powers that were too strong for him. In 1700 he acquiesced in another Inquisition attack on the woollen mills and eighteen important mill-owners were arrested. He recognised the growing importance of Brazil and was lucky when São Paulo backwoodsmen struck gold in the interior in 1697. In the next thirty years Portugal gained so much from the gold trade that it could temporarily abandon the search for innovations in production. The new wealth meant that the crown also had adequate revenues for domestic expenditure and could dispense with the calling of parliaments. The parliamentary cortes was not summoned again until 1822 after the outbreak of the Portuguese Revolution which followed on the heels of the French Revolution. Portuguese absolutism, which had failed to take root in

15   The Count of Ericeira was one of several outstanding modern political economists to attempt to reform the productive capacity of Portugal, but his limited success led to his suicide in 1690.

the 1660s, became so well established in the eighteenth century that the king's ministers were said to have greater authority than those of Frederick of Prussia, the archetypal enlightened despot.

The most lasting feature of Portugal's turn-of-the-century financial diplomacy, however, came with the signing of the Methuen Treaties of 1703. The antecedents of the Methuen Treaties went back to 1353 when a commercial treaty was signed between the ports of Oporto and London. This was twenty years before a royal treaty was agreed between Edward III of England and Ferdinand of Portugal and thirty-three years before the Treaty of Windsor and the dynastic marriage which gave birth to the royal princes who launched Portugal on its imperial career of overseas expansion. The eighteenth century sequels to the old alliance were both strategic and economic. Paul Methuen negotiated the military treaty on 16 May 1703. It gave England an entry to Portugal at a time when the Bourbon dynastic alliance of France and Spain appeared to threaten English access to the continent. The more important and lasting commercial treaty was signed by John Methuen on 27 December 1703. In article two of the treaty Queen Anne of England agreed that

her sacred Majesty of Great Britain be obliged in her own Name, and in the Name of her Successors, at all times to admit into England, Wines gathered from the vineyards belonging to the Portugal Dominions, as that at no time, whether there be Peace or War between the Kingdoms of England and France, any more shall be demanded for such wines, directly or indirectly, on account of Customs or Imposts, or upon any other Account whatsoever, than what shall, after deducting a third part of the Customs or Impost, be demanded from a like quantity of French Wine, whether such Wines shall be imported in Great Britain in Pipes, Hogsheads or any other vessels; but if at any time this Diminution of Duties, to be made aforesaid, shall in any manner be attempted, and the same shall be infringed, it shall be right and lawful for his sacred Majesty of Portugal to prohibit again Woollen Cloths and other Woollen Manufactures of England.

Cited in Carl A. Hanson, *Economy and Society in Baroque Portugal*
1668–1703 (Macmillan, London, 1981).

To have secured the Methuen Treaty was a coup of considerable importance for Portugal. Wine sales to England, which had fluctuated according to the availability of alternative French wines, were now assured of preferential entry. The Lisbon government could be sure

16   Sir Paul Methuen, depicted here by Joseph Highmore, and his father John Methuen negotiated one of the most famous commercial treaties of all time in 1703, thereby linking lastingly the economies of Portugal and Britain.

of regular exports to balance its imports and the landed interests could concentrate on wine production secure in the knowledge that they had a market. Opponents of modernisation saw the triumph of their policy of favouring a safely traditional monoculture. The treaty was by no means unequally favourable to Portugal, however, and England gained unhindered sales of textiles and clothing in a small but significant market where there was no longer a significant local industry to be outclassed and underpriced. Furthermore the wine and wool agreement also provided outlets for English cloth in the Atlantic colonies. The Methuen Treaty itself lasted until 1810, by which time the armies of Napoleon and Wellington had invaded Portugal, but the partnership between Britain and Portugal, for better or for worse, in sickness and in health, lasted very much longer.

3

The golden age and the earthquake in the eighteenth century

The golden age of modern Portugal dawned with the eighteenth century. King Pedro lived on until 1706 to witness the first ten years of Brazilian mining prosperity but it was his successor John V who reigned over the great flowering of Portuguese art and culture. Architecture blossomed as it had done under the first colonial empire of King Manuel in the early sixteenth century. Royal palaces and noble manor houses mirrored the splendour which Spain had built from its Latin American mining revenues. A small cultured élite became conversant with the world of learning and built fine libraries. Diplomats and even members of the royal family travelled through Europe and acquired cosmopolitan tastes. Churches were lavished with gilded carvings and ornamental decoration. The aristocracy ostentatiously rode in carriages wearing their finest robes. But the wealth of the few was matched by the poverty of the many. Peasants lived in almost feudal conditions of dependency. Fine palaces were not reflected in improvements to domestic and rural housing. The flowering of aristocratic learning was not mirrored by any development of public education or popular literacy. The Portuguese church remained one of the most conservative in Catholic Europe and continued to stifle open enquiry. The economy remained tied to Britain in a way which inhibited the broadening of the industrial base. Subsistence and survival were the hallmark of popular experience throughout the 'golden age'. Social and economic change did not begin to affect Portugal until the easy years of Brazilian gold were over and the great Lisbon earthquake of 1755 had destroyed the commercial heart of the metropolis.

Early eighteenth-century high society revolved around the palace on the great riverside square at Lisbon. Despite the political tensions which divided the crown and the nobility the royal apartments were crowded with suppliants and foreign visitors longed to be presented at court. Orders of precedence were regulated by the most stringent etiquette and the king became a remote and austere figure. The grandees usually numbered a few dukes, a dozen marquises and thirty-odd earls. Below them came the lesser nobility and thousands of impoverished knights of such militant orders of chivalry as the Order of Christ. Nobility of the blood was much prized but social mobility was possible and judges, generals and men of letters could acquire noble status. Men of rank spent much of their time dining at the homes of their equals and exchanging social and political gossip. They also engaged, incognito, in less innocent pleasures such as visiting the exuberant African dances of Lisbon's slaves and lusting after pretty black girls. White women of high society were severely secluded from public gaze and protected with passionate jealousy by their male guardians. Men of wealth sometimes took an official mistress until a socially compatible wife became available. Fortunate mistresses were given a pension when discarded, and lifelong security of residence in a convent, while their children could become incorporated into their father's social class. The Lisbon élite were fashion-conscious and liked to be seen in clothes of the latest Paris design. The king was said to possess more clothes than all the fashion houses of Lisbon put together. In order to keep their costumes clean in the narrow streets which served as drains and latrines the beautiful ones were carried in litters, curtained off from the popular gaze. Churchmen also had their bearers, coaches and escorts when they went out wining and dining. The greatest festival of the year was Corpus Christi when the city was immaculately cleaned and even society women were allowed to parade in the street to see the king, the queen and the cardinal ride by. About once a year gentile society also visited the church of Saint Vincent for one of the Inquisition's show trials. The condemned men and women of whatever rank were paraded through the streets and at dusk those sentenced

17   Contemporary engraving of a large crowd assembled in front of the waterfront palace in Lisbon to witness the burning of victims of the Inquisition.

to death were burnt at the stake to demonstrate that the church was still mightier than the state.

The central pillar of Portugal's eighteenth-century wealth and privilege was Brazilian gold discovered in the late 1690s. The alluvial deposits of the inland plateau attracted a gold rush of white planters and their black slaves. By 1700 the lawless frontier camps were washing 50,000 ounces of gold a year. Five years later the winnings amounted to 600,000 ounces of gold a year and the Portuguese empire was for the second time one of the world's great gold-producing enterprises. The mining industry stimulated the whole economy of Brazil. Cattle ranchers thrived on the supply of meat and leather to the mines and exported their surplus to Europe. The whaling industry supplied local cooking oil and also contributed to export revenue. Tobacco planters saw their market expand both in the mines and abroad when mine owners sent tobacco rolls to West Africa to buy new slaves for the diggings. Although the slavers lost some business when the Spanish slave supply contract was awarded to France in 1701, a contraband trade across South America continued to flourish. The sugar industry suffered from the loss of labour which emigrated to the mines, but survived with fresh imports from Africa. Such was the prosperity of Brazil that the Portuguese royal family, deemed to be the wealthiest in Europe, contemplated moving the court to Rio de Janeiro and forsaking the impoverished European half of its empire. The idea took root but was not implemented until a hundred years later.

The expansion of the Brazilian economy had one overriding effect on the broad mass of the Portuguese population in Europe. This was the opportunity to emigrate. In the sixteenth century Portugal had paid for its first empire, in Asia, with the export of migrants. In the twentieth century Portugal built its third empire, in Africa, on emigration rather than investment. In between these two cycles of migration the second empire, in America, was also based on the flow of fortune-seeking wanderers. The colonial population rose from one million in 1636 to two million in 1732 and three million in 1801. Eighteenth-century white emigration to Brazil did not match the forced African slave migration in terms of numbers but the flow of land-starved peasants from north Portugal opened a lasting demographic safety valve for the mother country. Portuguese emigration also ensured that, in spite of the growing economic influence of Britain in South America, the culture, language, religion and gastronomic tastes of Brazil became strikingly Portuguese and remained so after independence.

The Portuguese monarchy benefited from the Brazilian cornucopia in many different ways. The old balance of payments problem was solved for nearly two generations and did not again present a serious crisis until the 1760s. The taxation of growing colonial trade meant that alternative sources of domestic revenue did not have to be approved by the cortes and parliament was not summoned again for more than a century once gold began to flow into Lisbon. John V was able to create an absolutist regime superficially similar to that of the much wealthier kingdom of France. His personal rule contrasted sharply with the incipient parliamentary democracy of Britain. With such wealth he could afford to neglect all the old structural problems of Portugal's domestic economy. Impoverished agriculture, inadequate transport and minimal industrial development

18 This blue-tiled mural of 1730 shows the way Lisbon's houses and garden terraces rose steeply from the boatyards behind the waterfront towards the Alfama quarter of the city.

were ignored so long as corn and cloth could be imported. Even the merchant navy could be neglected when foreign sailors could be hired to man and defend the great fleets. Every problem in Portugal was temporarily solved by the king's gift of a little basket of gold coins bearing his effigy. The court of King John concentrated on pomp and ceremony while the English expatriates in Portugal turned their hands to commerce.

One of the lasting features of the golden age was a legacy of public works. In Coimbra the university library was rebuilt with the most ostentatious gilt decorations. The Braganza family seat out in the plains beyond the river was rebuilt to palatial standards. The city of Lisbon commissioned engineers to build a huge Roman-style aqueduct to bring fresh water from the hills on 200-foot stone pillars astride the valley. The city fathers tried unsuccessfully to get the king to finance the project but were able to raise the money from taxes on the popular consumption of meat, wine and olive oil in the golden city. The king himself was concerned with an even more

19   The palace-convent of Mafra was built in partial imitation
of the Escorial in Spain and reflected the piety and prosperity
of Portugal in the golden age of eighteenth-century Brazilian
mining.

spectacular architectural initiative, the building of his great palace
complex at Mafra. It was modelled on the Escorial in Spain and
was similarly built out in the countryside, far from the pressures
of the urban mob. The elegant design of the suites and courtyards
was matched by the costliness of the furnishings in more than 1,000
rooms. The scale of the buildings and of the formal gardens was
stupendous in relation to the impoverished countryside around it.
The edifice included a magnificent baroque monastery with a church
fitting to the royal estate. The Braganzas did not want to seem less
pious than their Spanish neighbours and therefore integrated the
religious house into the royal apartments in the manner that had
been favoured by Philip II. Eighteenth-century sceptics like Voltaire
poured rationalist scorn on the project and hinted that King John
fantasised about having nuns as mistresses. To the people of the district, however, the roped gangs of forced labourers and the military
regiment which controlled them provided a generation of employment opportunities, particularly in the servicing of the 7,000 carts
and waggons and the feeding of draught animals.

The wealth which flowed from Brazil was so great that it had to be carefully protected against pirates and smugglers. Portuguese mariners were both the practitioners of piracy and its victims. Traditionally Barbary corsairs captured rich Christians for ransom and poor ones as slaves but in the eighteenth century they also aspired to capture whole treasure fleets from Brazil. Competing Portuguese sea beggars used the Atlantic islands rather than the Moroccan ports for their predatory raids on royal shipping. Naval men-of-war, some of them supplied by Britain, were hired to protect the convoys as they approached the Azores and entered European waters. The danger was so acute that rich passengers to Lisbon were advised to carry a spare passport issued by a government friendly to the Muslim nations. From the crown's point of view, however, smuggling was an even greater problem than piracy. In 1697 the trade in brazilwood, the dye-giving wood which gave the country its name, was turned into a royal monopoly in an effort to impose greater control over the south American sea captains. The restriction was ineffectual and ships' crews continued to evade duty on private cargoes of all kinds, if necessary by bribing customs officers to close their eyes. The royal tobacco monopoly was also regularly breached by traders who hid rolls of tobacco in barrels of molasses. Tobacco duty was further evaded by the introduction of tobacco growing into Portugal itself. On a single day one remote nunnery in north Portugal was recorded as selling 250 pounds of illicit tobacco grown behind its secluding walls. In the south muleteers who were hired to take colonial tobacco over the mountains to Spain were often diverted to sell their packs untaxed on the home market. When parliament met for the last time in 1697 an attempt was made to impose a defence tax on tobacco. The scheme failed and instead the crown farmed the raising of tobacco revenue out to a consortium of merchants, threatening all smugglers with five years' deportation to the pestilential coast of Angola.

Gold soon eclipsed tobacco as the prime source of royal revenue but the collection of duty was just as difficult. All gold dust was supposed to be coined or cast as ingots under royal supervision at the mine head so that one-fifth could be put aside for the crown. Smuggling, however, was so notorious that in 1705 it was estimated that only 5 per cent of gold production, rather than 20 per cent, reached the treasury. The most successful smugglers were monks immune from government searches who hid their money belts beneath their habits. The thieving priesthood was alleged to operate on such a scale that all churchmen were for a time expelled from the mining district of Brazil. Gold was also smuggled to other parts of the Americas and sold tax-free to other European buyers. This overland contraband further deprived the crown of local revenue with which to finance an effective customs force. During the gold rush government control deteriorated even further when civil war broke out on the mines between camps of Portuguese immigrants who had come through north Brazil and Paulistas from south Brazil who had discovered the mines in the first place. In 1708 the governor of Rio de Janeiro invaded the mining province with his own local troops and established a rudimentary political and fiscal order. Mining continued to prosper but the ultimate beneficiary was neither Brazil nor Portugal but Britain.

During the peak years of mining the trade deficit between Portugal and Britain rose from half a million pounds sterling in the 1720s to 1 million pounds in the 1750s. This deficit had to be paid in bullion. Although the Portuguese wine trade had been greatly favoured by the Methuen Treaty and rose to account for 90 per cent of Portugal's own exports, the income could never cover the escalating cost of imports. Payment for English worsteds, bays and serges exceeded the wine revenue, quite apart from the cost of timber, barrel staves, fish, rice, maize and other supplies from British North America. Portuguese agricultural exports were also insufficient to pay for the 'invisible' earnings of the English at Lisbon and Oporto. Both the cod trade and the textile trade were based on credit transactions which cost a generous if not usurious rate of interest. Shipping services also earned Britain handsome invisible earnings. In little over half a century 25 million pounds worth of bullion was carried to Britain to balance the international ledger.

The shortest bullion route to England became the regular packet to Falmouth which used fast ships to evade corsairs. The mid-January packet in 1741 would have been a fine prize with its £28,000 of gold carried on behalf of sixty-one clients. In one year during the 1760s Falmouth imported Brazilian gold worth £895,000. The ships were normally declared immune from search in order to overcome the curious technicality that bullion exports from Portugal had been illegal since 1325 except at times of serious grain shortage. The continued illegality of bullion exports enabled Portuguese excise officers to harass foreign traders when it suited the purposes of the crown, and even to confiscate whole cargoes. To avoid such loss small trading houses used legitimate bills of exchange for their remittances, but the larger English firms, backed by the consul and the Factory, continued to take the risk of sending bullion. For greater security they sometimes hired vessels of the royal navy for their transactions and paid the skipper a commission. Portuguese gold coin circulated freely in eighteenth-century Britain as it did in the rest of Europe.

The great imperial prosperity of Portugal was first threatened thirty years after the mineral revolution when the most accessible of Brazil's gold mines were becoming exhausted and the cost of new production was rising. Fortunately for those who thrived on the colonial nexus a new, though equally transitory, source of wealth was uncovered when Brazil found that it had significant deposits of diamonds. The diamond trade added to the glitter of the court and to the traditional colonial revenue which enabled the day of reckoning to be postponed. The diamond trade came to be monopolised by The Netherlands' consul in Lisbon who organised shipment to the diamond houses of Amsterdam which specialised in cutting and polishing. Mineral wealth continued to sustain the crown until after John V died in 1750. Thereafter it was the ministers of his successor, Joseph I, who had to address the old problems of enhancing Portugal's domestic wealth when the Brazilian trade became less bountiful. Before they began to do so, however, the whole international trade of Portugal was severely shaken by the Lisbon earthquake of 1755. The cataclysm destroyed the English Factory, flooded the Customs House and burnt out the centre of the city.

The Lisbon earthquake was the most shattering natural phenomenon to disturb Europe's peace of mind in the eighteenth century. The great thinkers of the enlightenment debated its causes and consequences. The church wondered why it should have begun during mass on All Saints' Day and crushed so many worshippers. Merchants panicked at the loss of their coin hoards under the rubble. The royal family fled to the country and camped out for weeks, not daring to shelter under a fixed roof. Fires swept through the city for days after the last shocks had subsided. A young nun, Kitty Witham, sent a moving account of her ordeal to her mother in England:

I was washing the tea things when the Dreadfull afair hapned. itt began like the rattleing of Coaches, and the things befor me danst up and downe upon the table, I look about me and see the Walls a shakeing and a falling down then I up and took to my heells, with Jesus in my mouth, and to the quire I run, thinking to be safe there, but there was no Entranc but all falling rownd us, and the lime and dust so thick there was no seeing. I mett with some of the good Nuns they Cryed Outt run to the low garden, I ask where the rest was, they sayde there, so Blessed be his holy Name we all mett together, and run no further, we was all as glad to see one another alive and well as can be exprest. We spent the day in prayers, but with a great deal of fear and aprehension, as we had shakes and trembles all that day and night, and in fine ever since, only God knows how and when itt will end, last night we had a vere sharp one which renewed our fright vere much. We layde under a pair tree, covered with a Carpett, for Eight days, I and some others being so vere frighted every time the wind blode the tree, I thought we was going, so could not possible rest there, so we went to the Open air and slept there with much Pleasure, then the good fathers made us anothr little place with sticks and Coverd with Matts, where we some of us rested there a few Nights with the two fathers who came to us that Morning and glad to see us all alive as we was to see them. We have got a Wooden houes made in the garden, where the two good fathers and aboute half of us lives and lays there, but we lye in our Cloes I have never lain without my Cloes since All Saints. Which I find vere Uncomfortable but I beg God to accept it as a small Pennance. There is a bell that is rung att five a clock by them that has Currage to lay above, for those that has a mind to go to Mattins, if we have no fright in the Night by any Shock which we have some times then we dar not go and iff not we go, our Convent stands so hye that we have two and thirty stone steps to goe up to itt, Out of five and thirty Cells we have not One that we can lye in, till they are Repaird, the Church door has never been Opend Nor Mass sayde in itt since, tis so full of Rubish, as also the Quire and Refectory and the Kitchen entirely downe, so we must dow as well as we can till itt pleases All mighty God to send us a forturn, for I heard say we can take no more without. Them that has seen Lisbon before this dreadful Calamity and to see itt now would be greatly shockt the Citty is Nothing but a heep of Stones caused by the Great fier tis Callculated above forty thousand was destroyed and one the most terrible things that hapened was this, that many poor Souls Inclosed in the Ruings not Killd, but Could not gett out so some was burnt alive and Others dyed of humger . . . Sir Henry Franklen an acquaintance of Mr Killinghale was going in his shayz and percevd the houses to fall, he Jump out and a house fell upon him, he gett out throu some little hole and see a good many alive in a Nother street,

20 Contemporary drawing of the scene of devastation following the Lisbon earthquake.

he had Portugues to say Vene, that is Come hear, so saved them all, he left his shaze in the street broake, his Servants and horses killd.
        Cited in Rose Macaulay, *They Went to Portugal* (London, 1946)
                                                                pp. 269–70.

The suffering of the English nuns was matched by that of the whole population of Lisbon. Each section of society responded in its own fashion. The Inquisition was concerned lest its victims should escape during the calamity. Prisoners awaiting interrogation in the dungeons of its devastated palace were tied to the backs of mules and packed to Coimbra to be locked away once more while other convicts were given a free pardon. The wealthy bought passages on ships in the river to send their families abroad for safety. Foreigners crowded into houses and gardens on the residential hill around the embassies which had been spared the fire. Looters and arsonists were summarily hanged. Merchants raked through the ashes of their shops and warehouses for surviving valuables. Bankers refused to honour any bills and stopped all credit transactions. Portuguese retailers in the lower city lost all their cloth, most of which they had

obtained on credit from members of the English Factory. The Factory
members themselves lost virtually everything, though they managed
to obtain food which they offered to the king to ensure his goodwill.
The Customs House and the India House were destroyed so that no
new trade could be legitimately conducted. The English merchants
went to visit the king's minister and asked that the Customs House
be rebuilt as a matter of urgency. They were politely turned away
and told that humanitarian relief must take precedence. In order to
avert famine the Newfoundland cod fleet was seized by the government for emergency food distribution, to the heartless chagrin of the
English merchants who had been expecting it. When the expatriate
community did its reckoning it established that most of the British
victims of the earthquake had been 'unknown' Irish workers. The
middle-class section of English society acknowledged the death of
only forty-nine women and twenty-nine men. Within six months the
Factory was functioning again and priding itself on having stolen a
march on its foreign rivals during the emergency.

The immediate work of rehabilitation was undertaken by members of the church and the nobility. The illegitimate sons of John
V proved generous in their concern. The patriarchal church kept
priests at their posts so that the dead would be properly buried and
the living comforted. One of the royal dukes took responsibility
for law and order, calling up troops and strengthening the sea defences against pirates. The new king himself proved wise and active
in crisis management and the flight of panicked refugees was eventually stemmed. The most dramatic long-term consequence of the
Lisbon earthquake was the decision to completely rebuild the centre
of the lower city on a grid pattern of the type adopted in the new
cities of Spanish America. The royal palace on the waterfront had
been damaged beyond repair and a huge new square was planned
with an equestrian statue of Joseph I in the middle and the royal
apartments and government offices around three sides. Behind the
square the commercial and residential section of the city was to be
laid out in regular patterns. In order to rebuild on the mud churned
up by the tidal wave that accompanied the earthquake thousands
of timber pylons were brought from northern Europe as foundations. On top of these posts fine multistorey stone buildings were
designed in a regular architectural style. Lisbon was intended to be

the finest city in Europe. The surviving wealth of Brazil, although declining, was expected to finance the great vision. The execution of the project, however, was slow and the magnificent city was very far from finished by the time Joseph I died in 1777 and his famous chief minister, the Marquis of Pombal, fell from grace. In the meantime huge shanties had sprung up in the spaces around the seven hills of Lisbon. That is where the plebeian victims of fire and flood lived while the nobility, the oligarchy and the priesthood restored their stone dwellings.

The Lisbon earthquake had repercussions which went far beyond municipal reconstruction. Theological recriminations of some virulence broke out as victims of the catastrophe searched anxiously through the ruins for their favourite relics, crucifixes and madonnas. Preachers instilled an exaggerated fear of sin into their parishioners to the dismay of a government anxious to avoid further panic. One outspoken Jesuit accused the government of adopting futile palliatives when men should be saving their souls before yet greater punishment be inflicted upon them. His half-crazed ministry made him into a popular local 'saint'. To stop his preaching he was handed to the Inquisition who made a public display of his 'heresies'. In 1761 he was paraded round Lisbon by torchlight and his ashes were scattered at sea. Such virulence of theological sentiment in a country still prone to the twin forces of piety and bigotry attracted foreign attention. Voltaire had been particularly struck by the devastation that the earthquake had caused. He wrote, though cautiously avoiding religious scandal, about the doubt which it cast on the doctrine of a well-ordained world. In his satirical novel *Candide* the hero visited Lisbon during the earthquake, and suffered all the hardships of the natural catastrophe, as well as the persecutions of the Inquisition, but still emerged believing with smiling irony that all was for the best in the best possible of all worlds. Voltaire is worth quoting for his exaggerated view of Portuguese society at the time:

After the earthquake, which had destroyed three-quarters of Lisbon, the Portuguese pundits could not think of any better way of preventing total ruin than to treat the people to a splendid *auto da fé*, for the University of Coimbra had declared that the spectacle of a number of people being ceremonially burnt over a slow fire was an infallible way of preventing an earthquake. So they seized for this purpose a Basque who had married his

21 Lisbon is dominated by the high-walled Moorish castle captured by crusaders in 1147. The square-towered cathedral lies behind the arcade of the waterfront royal palace, rebuilt after the earthquake in 1755. The skyline church is São Vicente in which the 1445 Nuno Gonçalves altar painting of Prince Ferdinand was found.

godmother, and also two Portuguese caught out in the Jewish trick of refusing to eat the bacon part of a larded chicken. Pangloss and his pupil Candide were also both arrested at the dinner in the ruins, one for having spoken imprudently, and the other for having listened approvingly. Both of them were marched off and imprisoned separately in extremely cold cells where there was not the slightest danger of their suffering any inconvenience from the sun. A week later they were each dressed up in a *sanbenito* [a heretic's robe] with a paper mitre as a hat. Candide's costume was decorated with flames pointing downwards and devils without tails or claws; Pangloss's devils had both tails and claws, and his flames were shooting upwards. Thus clothed, they were led off in a procession and listened to a very moving sermon, followed by some nice music in counterpoint. Candide was flogged in rhythm with the chanting; the Basque and the two men who wouldn't eat bacon were burnt, and Pangloss was hanged, though that was not the normal practice at these ceremonies. The same day there was another tremendous and very noisy earthquake that did great damage.

Cited in T. D. Hendrick, *The Lisbon Earthquake* (London, 1956).

In London the reactions to the news from Lisbon were less sardonic than those of the French philosophers. A shipment of picks, shovels, boots, rice, smoked herring and emergency rations was immediately sent from Portsmouth. The humane gesture was quickly followed by anxiety about the financial loss as the merchant class in Britain hummed with anecdotes about whose fortunes had been tied to the Lisbon Factory house. The wife of a future Archbishop of York was but one individual who lost £7,000 in Lisbon. But the greatest reaction was one of sorrow, for many people in Britain knew Portugal far better than any other foreign country. Portugal had been an ally for several centuries and was deemed familiar and friendly territory, however much the Portuguese might feel exploited and patronised by the quasi-colonising attitudes of the English who lived among them. Distress over the earthquake led the Royal Society to initiate research into the scientific understanding of seismology. Foreign curiosity, however, was also tinged with fear as powerfully expressed in Germany by Goethe, who had been six years old at the time. He vividly retained a childhood memory of the 'Demon of Fright' which spread horror through the land and cast doubt on the concept of an all-powerful and merciful God.

The chief minister of Portugal's King Joseph, known by his later title of Pombal, succeeded in getting the history of Lisbon rewritten after the earthquake. Rival claimants to credit in the rehabilitation

of the city were banished and Pombal used the event to foster a
new historical tradition in which he was cast in the role of the great
and omniscient benefactor. Within a decade of the cataclysm it was
recorded that it had been Pombal who had averted God's wrath,
preserved the king's person, punished the traitors, restored commerce, encouraged the arts, cleared the ruins and rebuilt the city.
He even had the stone inscription on the great aqueduct changed to
give credit to his royal masters rather than to the citizens of Lisbon.
The truth was more varied but Pombal had nonetheless become the
central figure of Portuguese politics and the king, his royal patron,
sank into the shadows.

Pombal was one of the most innovative rulers that Portugal ever
had, though his dictatorial methods reflected much of the harshness of eighteenth-century absolutism. He belonged to a tradition of
Portuguese scholars, diplomats and politicians who had lived abroad
and were familiar with the European enlightenment. They became a
noblesse de robe uncomfortably balanced between the upper bourgeoisie and the lesser nobility. They were known as the 'alienised'
élite and were never popular with the archaic nobility of traditional
society. Nor were they approved by the privileged English merchants
of Lisbon and Oporto for they sought to develop a native merchant
class able to control the country's own destiny. During the golden
age their influence had been limited, though John V had been a far
more cultured man than the pious oaf that critics and historians
portrayed. Once the old king was dead the ambitious and patriotic
modernisers grasped their opportunities quickly, Pombal to the fore.

Pombal gained his influence at court with two advantages. The
first was that he had married into the Austrian nobility during his
service in Vienna and was known to Portugal's Austrian-born dowager queen. It was she who summoned him to take charge of foreign
affairs when her husband died. Pombal's second and in the long
run more influential advantage was that during his long posting to
London he had read widely among modern works of political
economy. He fully understood the strengths and weaknesses of the
intimate Portuguese commercial relationship with Britain. He also
recognised that any economic innovations would have to be approached slowly and tactfully. One of his correspondents wisely
advised him that all radical change had to be disguised in the most

22   The Marquis of Pombal was the authoritarian moderniser
who began the reconstruction of Lisbon after the earthquake
in 1755 and who encouraged the wine trade when colonial
revenues from Brazil began to wane.

conventional of institutional cloaks. Pombal was thus both informed
and cautious when he embarked on his quarter of a century of increasing power as minister to Joseph I. He was also hardworking
and ambitious as well as taciturn and stubborn.

Although Pombal recognised that his economic plans would have
to be slowly implemented, he also knew from seventeenth-century
experience that the greatest obstacle to change would come from

the traditional nobility. These arch-defenders of tradition had continued to tolerate the heretical but necessary English enclaves of Lisbon and Oporto but were much more fearful of the emergence of a native merchant class. One of Pombal's most important steps, once he had secured the king's approval, was therefore to confront the power of the aristocracy in order to make way for the growth of a more influential bourgeoisie. This he did by dividing the nobility against itself. Some nobles were given preferment and favours which made them loyal dependants of the monarchy and of its secretariat. Others, on the other hand, were singled out for persecution of a barbarity almost unequalled until the executions of the French Revolution thirty years later. The attack on the nobility began in 1758 when it was announced that the king was 'indisposed' and that his queen had assumed the regency.

Months later the king's indisposition was presented to the public by the government's propaganda machine as being the result of an assassination plot by disaffected aristocrats who had failed to get Pombal dismissed. Pombal directed his revenge first of all at the Duke of Aveiro whose palace was destroyed and whose garden was strewn with salt to symbolise sterility. He then turned on the Tavora family whose hostility to the crown was probably associated with wounded honour, resulting from the king's amorous indiscretions, rather than with policies of state. To Pombal the Tavoras were a suitable target for casting down the influence of the great families of the grandees. In a carefully orchestrated display of unbridled power the Marquis of Tavora was broken on the wheel in medieval style while the marchioness was forced to witness the execution of her own children. The Tavora coat of arms was extinguished and chiselled from buildings. As the Pombal terror spread a thousand or more alleged enemies of the king and his minister were incarcerated in dungeons throughout Portugal and those that survived remained there for twenty years. Even the king's brother was not beyond Pombal's suspicion, and the illegitimate siblings were banished from society and politics and confined to a monastery. Lesser opponents were exiled to the colonies to deter any further opposition to the new dictatorship.

In a second step towards establishing an absolute despotism which would give him a free hand in adopting 'enlightened' reforms

Pombal attacked sections of the church. He began by driving the Jesuits from their traditional place of influence as confessors of the royal family. When the papal nuncio protested, Pombal threatened to cut all links with the Vatican and establish an autonomous national church in semi-Protestant style. The persecution of the Jesuits intensified until their monasteries and schools were closed, their colonial possessions were confiscated and eventually all their priests were expelled from Portuguese territory. Pombal's success in crushing one of the most influential forces in Catholic Europe spread to Spain and France where similar persecutions were launched. Ultimately the pope was forced to dissolve the whole Jesuit order, in part as the price for restoring Portuguese allegiance to Rome. Pombal set about replacing Jesuit education, including the university at Evora, with state education under his own control. A network of primary schools was envisaged to train government clerks and instil respect for the new state order. The scheme was never fully implemented, however, and the training of commercial clerks, who might compete with British ones, lagged far behind national requirements. At the university town of Coimbra the challenge to the church led to the arrest of the bishop and the reform of higher education allowed the dissemination of French philosophy. Science and mathematics were brought into the syllabus as part of the training for a new generation of high state functionaries and army engineers. Changes of an even more radical kind were proposed in medical and surgical education. But Pombal's great modernising vision, complete with a botanical garden and an astronomical observatory, depended on an unrealistic recruitment of the old legal and theological faculties. The promised enlightenment was constantly hampered by the inertia of a benighted past.

Pombal's social reforms designed to open the way to new economic prosperity went beyond the field of education. He recognised that one burden which held Portugal back was still the institutionalised persecution of all Portuguese of Jewish descent. He therefore outlawed racial discrimination and determined that New Christians should be given genuine legal equality with Old Christians. In order to carry out such a radical change he had to confront the Inquisition. This he did by virtually abolishing its church role and turning it into a state tribunal. Inquisitorial methods of social control were not discontinued but were in future used on behalf of the Pombal administration. The new victims of the interrogators were no longer industrial investors and commercial entrepreneurs accused of heresy, but alleged enemies of the state accused of treason. In addition to freeing Jews from their disabilities, Pombal freed blacks in Portugal from their slave status. He did so not out of liberal idealism or a commitment to the concept of wage incentives, but in order to stop colonial families from bringing slaves off the plantations of Brazil to Portugal as servants. Brazil remained the key to Portugal's international economy and could not afford to lose the scarce and expensive black labour which was occasionally taken away to work in Europe. Enhancing the agricultural wealth of Brazil, and gaining more control over it, became one of Pombal's attempted economic reforms.

One way in which Pombal sought to dominate the Portuguese and Brazilian economies was by licensing 'monopoly' trading companies which could be managed by loyal supporters of his king. Two of these companies were given Brazilian interests and to defend their aspirations Pombal restricted the free trade of independent commercial agents accustomed to going to Brazil as pedlars carrying merchandise obtained on credit from the English. By outlawing these 'flying agents' Pombal risked incurring the wrath of the English wholesalers, but he had done his research carefully and the measure did not injure the interests of powerful English firms but only those of minor middlemen with little political influence at the 'court' of the British consul. In founding his great companies Pombal hoped to foster an indigenous commercial bourgeoisie which could rival the influence of the nobility. His agents were not intended to encourage the rise of a radical petty bourgeoisie or foster innovative means of production but merely to channel licence fees and trading profits to the new middle-class politicians. The company bureaucrats who gained an insight into the functioning of the Brazil trade were particularly instructed to cream profits from it. Brazil was so important to Pombal that he sent his own brother there to take charge of company initiatives.

Pombal's commitment to extracting new personal and national wealth from Brazil was one source of his ardent conflict with the Jesuits. The Jesuit colonial territories stretched throughout the interior of Brazil from the Amazon to the River Plate. The missionaries had been the great rivals of the São Paulo backwoodsmen who had explored the interior in the seventeenth century and discovered the gold mines. In many instances the Jesuits had worsted the Paulistas in battle and built well-fortified villages for their native American subjects. Spanish and Portuguese Jesuits occasionally co-operated to gain advantage over their respective colonial governments. In 1750, for instance, Jesuits had violently opposed the transfer of the Uruguay missions from Spain to Portugal and had armed their subjects to resist. Pombal became increasingly fearful of Jesuit power and obsessed with the notion that the Jesuits were linked in an unholy conspiracy with the independent merchants whom he wished to suppress in favour of his own monopoly trading companies. Against this the Jesuits believed quite reasonably that Pombal's policy of imposing state control over the backlands and of fostering colonisation by encouraging European settlers to breed with aboriginal women, would lead to cruel exploitation and racial extermination. The open debate about colonising policy and wealth extraction in the far interior was less important, however, than the covert conflict over real control of the prosperous coastlands.

In addition to holding mission lands in the interior, the Jesuits of Brazil owned some of the richest plantations and most expensive urban real estate in South America. One of their Rio de Janeiro estates covered 100,000 acres and employed 1,000 slaves. They also owned seventeen sugar factories in the lowland plantation zones. Their managerial efficiency was the key to their success and the source of widespread jealousy and accusations of venality. The 600 ordained Jesuit priests were unpopular with the much more numerous priesthood of the secular branches of the church. Pombal's attack did not therefore seem like an attack on the church as a whole and indeed rival churchmen were among the first to denounce their Jesuit rivals. The steadfast Jesuit refusal to surrender their privileges and submit to state taxation led Pombal to expropriate their properties. These were then sold, often at low prices owing to the glut of newly available mission lands, to private buyers. The enriched landowners became a new source of political and social influence and speeded Brazil towards a sense of separate identity. Meanwhile in Lisbon Pombal little suspected that he was setting a long-term precedent for a much wider and more revolutionary dissolution of the monasteries in Portugal itself.

One reason why Pombal dispossessed the Brazilian Jesuits in favour of his new trading companies was an aspiration to limit the scale of English domination over the supply of Brazilian imports. In this he was seriously thwarted. In 1762 he was forced abruptly to reverse his anti-British stance when Spain unexpectedly invaded Portugal. The government hastily confirmed its attachment to the British alliance and called for a trained British army to defend Portugal's borders. The annual fleet to Brazil was held in Lisbon lest the royal family should suddenly find itself forced to flee to the Americas. Pombal curtailed proposals to extend state trading to areas of Brazil where it might cause offence to English interests. The sudden Spanish threat was so real that it caused him to move the Brazilian capital from Bahia to Rio de Janeiro for strategic reasons. He recalled how nearly Portugal had lost Brazil during the Spanish War of Succession when both French colonial interests in Guiana and Dutch merchant interests on the high seas had aspired to gain control and only the British alliance had saved Portugal's interests. Instead of curtailing British activity Pombal therefore embarked on a more modest programme of economic innovation.

The new viceroy of Brazil was encouraged to diversify agricultural production by planting coffee as an experimental new crop. A century later coffee outstripped all other produce and Brazil dominated the world supply. To minimise British imports he encouraged the growing of wheat, rice and flax. In the far north a colonial company revived the tradition of cotton planting and another stimulated the old tobacco trade. The very success of these Pombal initiatives, however, contained the seeds of long-term failure for Portugal. Brazil became wealthier and more self-reliant. Brazilians aspired to develop their own industries rather than supply raw materials to those of Portugal. The colonial nexus became increasingly strained and led to outbreaks of violence as Brazil moved slowly towards a declaration of independence in 1822.

Portugal's long-term difficulties in dominating the Brazil trade forced it to seek alternative niches in the Atlantic where it could enjoy an unhindered advantage. One such colonial market, where competition was not strong enough to exclude Portuguese shipping and investment, was Angola. In Angola the colonial state facilitated the sale of over-priced and protected commodities from Portugal and from the scattered remnants of Portugal's old empire in Indonesia (Timor), in India (Goa) and in China (Macau). Angola was also a market for rough wine which even the unquenchable British would not import. Whereas Brazil was rich enough to be selective in its manufactured tastes, and to choose British rather than Portuguese quality goods, Angola was a dumping ground for Portuguese products that were not competitive on the world market. Lisbon merchants who could not compete in supplying Brazil found a back door to Brazilian wealth via Africa and the slave trade. This trade was risky and not always very profitable, but it offered struggling national traders a limited prospect of capturing a share of Brazil's profits. British and French competition in the slave trade to Brazil was restricted until late in the eighteenth century by the unattractive profit margins and by their commitment to supplying the huge slave demand in their own colonies.

The initial success of the Lisbon merchants in dealing with eighteenth-century Brazil was due to their ingenuity in devising a 'slave bridge' across the South Atlantic on which they avoided personally bearing the highest risks. They out-manoeuvred their slave suppliers in the African ports by selling merchandise and transport services rather than by buying slaves outright. The slaves remained the property of the vendor until they reached Brazil. The Lisbon carriers received their payment in coin or in Brazilian credit notes. The risk of owning slaves who might die on the middle passage was thus avoided by Portuguese entrepreneurs. Far from seeing the loss of slaves as a risk, these 'merchants of death' saw potential advantage in high slave mortality. The more rapidly slaves died, the sooner fresh ones would be needed, thus further extending the market for their shoddy commodities. The driving force of this South Atlantic system was credit. In Africa the Lisbon trade goods were given out on credit to brokers recruited among exiled deserters and criminals who had been shipped from Europe or Asia to the Angolan ports. They in turn gave commodities on credit to caravan leaders who went up-country to meet the slave catchers at the great inland slave fairs. Once the slaves reached Brazil credit was again the driving force. Agricultural estates were so deep in debt that whatever the state of the sugar market planters had little option but to go on buying slaves and producing sugar to pay off old borrowings.

The Lisbon trade with Angola was dominated by two interest groups. The 'British' group were primarily concerned with ensuring that Brazil had enough slaves to maintain mineral and crop production. They received payment in gold and cotton and were loosely linked to a pro-British faction at court. Their rivals were associated with the 'French faction' at court and preferred payment in Peruvian silver which could be sold at a premium in India for finished cotton goods. They also accepted payment in sugar which sold well in the kingdoms of the Mediterranean which had no tropical colonies of their own. Despite competition between them, both trading traditions collaborated to keep the price of commodities in Africa high to the overall advantage of Europeans as opposed to Africans. The Lisbon merchants also furthered their advantage by manipulating their government connections and relying on friendly royal courts to favour their cause in any credit litigation. Not all the traders to Angola, however, belonged to these established traditions of well-connected merchants. Occasional adventurers mounted expeditions to Angola and were castigated as gun runners and smugglers accused of buying slaves from embezzlers fleeing from their creditors to the small out-ports of Africa. Such outlaws offended against the 'orderly' Lisbon slave trade.

One advantage which the regular Lisbon traders had traditionally enjoyed was the opportunity to bid for the tax contract associated with the slave trade in Angola. In Spain the better known though rather different *asiento* slave trading licence was prized by foreigners as much for the opportunities it provided to smuggle non-perishable goods into the Spanish empire as for the right to transport highly perishable slave cargoes. In Portugal the advantage of bidding for the 'tax farm' was not only a comparable trading advantage, but it also gave the holder preference when calling in debts. It also conferred a crown monopoly in the ivory trade and a small profit margin on the collecting of crown taxes. These benefits were limited, however, to a six-year term and so encouraged the contractor to flood the market with goods while he held the advantage, regardless of inflation. Contractors also granted themselves a loading advantage on waiting ships and contravened the legislation on tight packing of cargoes to get more of their own slaves away to Brazil quickly.

Overcrowding became one of the most visible of the contractors' abuses and was one of the justifications used by Pombal to attack the system and create new openings in the slave trade for his protégés. Restructuring the slave trade in favour of his new companies was not, however, one of Pombal's more successful schemes. Although the two chartered Brazil companies gained a small segment of the Angolan trade, they could not compete with their independent Rio de Janeiro rivals. Worse still slave suppliers resisted Portuguese attempts to squeeze African profits and developed new outlets to British ports north of Angola. Only in the late eighteenth century, after Pombal had left office, did Portugal recover its primacy as a slaving power but by then Britain was on the eve of abandoning the slave trade and moving towards its suppression.

While Lisbon specialised in slave trading from Africa, Oporto became the centre of the wine trade to England in the eighteenth century. Portuguese table wine was not ideal for the English market but it was a more acceptable alternative to French claret than Spanish substitutes and the supply was less liable to political interference. Much of the wine went to the port of London, but some was also shipped direct to King's Lynn, to Hull or to Bristol. The Oporto wine trade was so successful that by the 1720s English wholesalers were shipping 25,000 pipes a year, four times the wine shipments out of Lisbon. English vintners rode through the small peasant vineyards of the Douro valley on horseback testing the vintage and buying wine for cash carried by their armed escorts. In the 1730s the Oporto wine trade changed when English wine merchants began to lace the best Douro wines with brandy. The resulting fortified wines were kept in great cellars on the south bank of the river for two or three years and then sold as 'port wine' shipped mature rather than drunk young as in the past. The profits were greatly increased and the economic power of the English enhanced. They were able to buy wine on credit, thus deferring payment on wines they had selected until they had been safely shipped down the dangerous river rapids and delivered to their cellars. Portuguese general merchants in the area were never able to accumulate the capital, or acquire the knowledge, to become producers of such fine wines. A merchant selling 4,000 pipes a year needed a capital of some £60,000 to fortify port even if he could buy fresh wine at only £7 per pipe. In the 1760s this enclave of foreign prosperity attracted the attention of Pombal in his endeavour to create a national merchant class and to enhance the Portuguese share of the profits on international trade.

Pombal's policy towards the port wine trade was a mixture of shrewd economics tempered with venal corruption. He implemented his policy through a wine company established in 1756. Pombal well understood that to enhance the national benefit from the wine trade he would need both to improve quality and to restrict supply. To do this he insisted that port wine production be confined to a *zone d'appellation controlée*, but he illegitimately included his own vineyards, which were far outside the Douro valley and on quite different soils, in the privileged production zone. To improve selection he insisted that farmers should specialise in either white or red production and no longer produce a mixed vintage as hitherto. The peasants of the north were also compelled to destroy all their elder trees to stop the traditional use of elder juice as a ruinous colouring agent. The use of fertilisers was banned, thus greatly reducing the farmers' yields but enhancing the flavour of the wine and the profits of the traders. Pressure on the English wine houses to use Portuguese brandy substitutes to fortify the wines did not succeed, however, and imported French brandy continued to be added to quality port wine. The Douro Wine Company never made a profit for its reluctant shareholders, many of whom were municipal or ecclesiastical authorities which had been compelled to invest their reserves in shares. It did, however, reward its administrators well and helped to build up Pombal's new middle class. It also enhanced the popularity of port wine as a society drink in the common-rooms of Oxford and Cambridge, thus increasing the incidence of gout among English dons.

The Douro Wine Company was the most influential, the most lasting and the most unpopular of Pombal's trading ventures. English high society in Oporto hated it and unjustly accused Pombal of being pathologically xenophobic. In truth it was Pombal's very pragmatism that enabled the English to survive and flourish in their fine suburban houses cut off from the natives by wrought-iron gates.

Successful English wine traders were even able to buy their own vineyards and become prosperous landowners. The great Factory House became an enclave of Anglo-Saxon culture and opulence where business was conducted in the greatest secrecy. At the other end of the city's social spectrum the local populace had a more genuine grievance when the wine company was given a monopoly in supplying common wine to the local taverns. The dictator spuriously alleged that the measure was designed to protect drinkers from substances injurious to health, although all recognised that the measure was designed to provide monopoly profits to his associates. Serious rioting took place and the local justice of the peace sympathised with the popular indignation. An unrelenting Pombal called up five army regiments to impose his will and arrested 400 alleged ringleaders. He subsequently claimed that only the merciful generosity of the king had limited the number of executions to thirty hangings, though the hapless judge was among them.

The success of the port wine trade did not trickle down to farmers who were excluded from the favoured production zone. Even within the zone some producers were forced to grub up their vines and plant olives when Pombal feared that excessive production might reduce prices. Elsewhere the production of ordinary Portuguese wines expanded without government encouragement but the quality deteriorated further. Even Brazilians began to buy contraband table wines from France or Spain because Portuguese wine was so rough. The old northern harbour at Viana, which had once had a thriving English community, lost its British consul and all but two of its expatriate trading houses. Farms in the green Minho province behind the harbour were forced to grow cabbages in place of vines. Peasants were driven to emigrate or to become casual labourers in the favoured Douro wine zone. As itinerant grape pickers they faced the competition of migrant workers from across the Spanish border who were willing to tolerate even more miserable conditions of pay, food and lodging.

Despite the relative success of the Atlantic empire and of the specialised port wine trade, Portugal remained a severely underdeveloped country in the 1760s. Pombal's efforts had benefited a few advantaged members of the lesser aristocracy and the urban middle class but elsewhere the landless remained landless and most rural landowners remained as cut off from market opportunities as ever. Mules were the standard pack animal, and even Coimbra was not linked to Lisbon by a track until 1798 when a diligence service was instituted but had to close for lack of business. In the north ox waggons became more plentiful but the highroad from Oporto to Braga was so muddy that it could take five days for a wheeled vehicle to cover the forty miles. Without post coaches the royal mail in Portugal was carried on long-distance footpaths and bridle-tracks. Pombal's one notable attempt at modernising the transport system was the construction of a short canal to his own vineyards. He was later accused, though not convicted, of having spent 6 million cruzados of public money, almost as much as the whole cost of the Lisbon aqueduct, on various improvements to his family properties. Private opulence was not matched by public investment, however, and even the great Douro River down which the best wine was brought remained an unimproved waterway subject to great hazards. Outside the areas of peasant subsistence the scarcity of food continued and foreign wheat from Italy or the Baltic made up 12 per cent of national consumption. In the poorest areas of the north peasants began to adopt the American potato as their staple but had no means of transporting it to market. In some of the wetter river valleys maize was introduced to improve grain yields but the 'maize revolution' was limited and localised. Portugal had not succeeded in ploughing its revenues into development and economic diversification by the time the recession of the 1760s descended on the country.

When foreign trade faltered late in the 1760s Pombal revived the old Portuguese projects for industrialisation which had been attempted by the Count of Ericeira a century before. Hitherto he had not been an innovator but only a redistributor of wealth who knew how to reward his supporters by controlling the production of others. Now he faced a balance of payments crisis which drove him to encourage the development of home industries and so save exchange on manufactured imports. An attempt was made to revive the long-persecuted woollen textile industry by importing looms from Britain. By the end of the century some 500 small woollen mills were functioning. An old silk industry for which impressive premises had been built above Lisbon in the previous reign was revived and attracted a relatively large workforce of 3,000 people. In Oporto a cotton spinning and weaving industry was encouraged though it did not prosper until the nineteenth century and ran into severe initial problems of competition with the cheap new textiles produced by advanced British technology. The industrial drive also sought to make Portugal less dependent on iron imports from Russia and Spain by setting up an iron foundry in Angola. Ambitious buildings were put up and named after Pombal's country seat but the Basque iron masters who were sent out to Africa succumbed to the malarial climate. The industrial programme, although more successful than the one which had been stifled by the Inquisition in the seventeenth century, remained marginal to the international realities of Portugal as a vine-growing monoculture.

In 1777 significant changes took place in Portugal. King Joseph died and his chief minister was relieved of office and told by Queen Maria I that there would be no place for him in the new administration. Political prisoners were released and exiles returned home. The cowed sections of the aristocracy regained some of their influence at court. Even the cruelly persecuted Tavora family was posthumously rehabilitated. The greatest beneficiary of Pombal's fall was the church which recovered its political ascendancy and tried to guide the increasingly pious queen in her policies. The great abbey of Alcobaça was thriving when visited by the wealthy English traveller Beckford at the end of the century. The conservative restoration was by no means as complete, however, and most of Portugal's new bureaucrats retained their posts though the policies established under Joseph I were modified when the pressure on government to maintain an interventionist role in economic affairs was eased by the ending of the European recession and the revival of the wine trade. To most Portuguese the reign of Maria demonstrated continuity rather than reform or restoration. Peasants continued to live at the lowest of standards and to pay a plethora of feudal-type dues to their landlords. Monasteries and country squires owned most of the windmills and forges and jealously preserved their monopoly over such essential rural services as corn milling and blacksmithing. Glimmerings of forthcoming change were mainly perceived by the still very small and predominantly urban middle class with access to new ideas and new opportunities.

23 Windmills with rotating roofs were equipped with open-necked pots which whistled to warn the miller when the wind was too strong and his sails needed trimming.

The most subversive ideas to reach Maria's Portugal came on the grain fleets from North America where the War of Independence threatened to spread ideas of democracy around the world. The political police that had emerged from the Inquisition took strenuous measures to stifle intellectual debate and to arrest potential dissidents. More acceptable foreign ideas came from the *ancien régime* of

France and brought a new neo-classical culture to the court. The old baroque styles of Spain gave way to a new art as seen in the queen's great palace of Queluz built to mirror Versailles, in sharp stylistic contrast to the palace of Mafra that John V had built. The middle class which Pombal had struggled so long to promote prospered moderately under Queen Maria when successful traders acquired country estates and took on noble pretensions. During the reign no fewer than thirty-four members of the high bourgeoisie were raised to the peerage. The new nobility, like the old, remained heavily dependent on the crown for its status. Even earldoms were not always granted in perpetuity but for one or two generations in order to preserve royal ascendancy. By ennobling the most influential members of the middle class the queen managed to forestall throughout her reign pressure from the commons for the calling of parliament. No Portuguese parliament was elected until after her death by which time the winds of change from Paris had hit Portugal and unleashed the Portuguese Revolution. Meanwhile the Lisbon government was strengthened by the modernisation of accountancy and by the creation of a ministry of finance alongside the three traditional secretaries of state responsible for the interior and home affairs, for war and foreign affairs and for the navy and the colonies. The rebuilt city was belatedly brought to order with a royal police force and safety was improved by the long overdue introduction of street lighting.

The last years of the eighteenth century saw the beginning of fundamental change spilling out from the city into the rural districts north and south of Lisbon. The indigenous trading class had grown to 80,000 strong and had begun to invest in neglected lands in the Estremadura and Alentejo provinces. They were more dynamic than the old noble landowners and enhanced their wealth by selling not only wine but also wheat, wool and olive oil. Craftsmen began to prosper too and 130,000 artisans supplied the market rather than being predominantly tied to aristocratic and religious patrons. Another change of long-term significance was the professionalisation of the armed forces. The ragged militias and personal battalions of the aristocratic estates were replaced by permanent regiments with formal ranks which recognised competence as well as social status. The promotion of career officers in what had been a noble profession created a military class which sometimes identified with the growing

merchant and bureaucratic élite. Officers also gained technical training designed for military defence but incidentally applicable to industrial projects. The new officers were later to play an important
role in the politics of revolution and some looked back on the temporarily disgraced Marquis of Pombal as their hero. Before the new
political age dawned, however, Napoleon seized Portugal in an effort
to complete his continental conquests and wrest the still lucrative
Brazilian empire from the economic clutches of the British.

4

Brazilian independence and the Portuguese Revolution

In 1807 the imperial army of France entered Portugal led by General Junot, one of Napoleon's favourite officers and his former ambassador at the Braganza court. Before the invaders reached Lisbon the royal family and numerous courtiers and camp-followers were evacuated by the British navy and taken for safe keeping to Brazil. The Lisbon bourgeoisie, and those sections of the nobility which remained behind, sensibly welcomed the French who ruled the city for some months before being driven out by a British expeditionary force. Further French and British invasions seriously impoverished the country and culminated in the establishment of a British military authority commanded by Viscount Beresford. The Portuguese royal family remained in Brazil and signed an Anglo-Portuguese treaty in 1810 which superseded the Methuen Treaty of 1703 and recognised direct access to Brazil by British traders, thus accelerating the drift towards Brazilian political independence. Ten years later restiveness at British military overrule in Portugal led to the outbreak of the Portuguese Revolution of 1820. This French-style revolution lasted intermittently for thirty-one years and only after the turbulence of civil war, terror, anti-clericalism and dictatorship, did the country settle to a constitutional monarchy closely linked to Victorian England. Brazil meanwhile broke away politically from Portugal in 1822 to become an autonomous 'empire' ruled by a Latin Americanised branch of the Braganza royal house. The former colony continued, however, to import slaves from Portuguese Africa until 1850 when policy changed and Brazil switched to satisfying all of its labour requirements with free white immigrants from Europe. Many of these came from the north of Portugal, thus maintaining the cultural and economic links between the two countries.

Before deciding to invade Portugal in 1807 Napoleon had signed a secret treaty with Spain laying out his plans for the future. He intended first of all to deprive the British of their last access to continental Europe as a reprisal for the economic blockade which Britain was trying to impose on France's continental empire. Next he proposed that Portugal should be comprehensively dismembered. The north would be turned into an autonomous Spanish protectorate and given to an Italian king whose territory Napoleon aspired to add to his personal domains. The south of Portugal, and the kingdom of the Algarve, were to be awarded to a Spanish prince who would be required to maintain an alliance with Spain. The midlands of Portugal including Lisbon were to be reserved for possible restitution to the house of Braganza subject to good conduct under French tutelage and an agreement that the British would surrender to Napoleon the fortress of Gibraltar which they had previously captured from Spain. This visionary plan for Iberian reorganisation also entailed a partitioning of the Portuguese colonies with the king of Spain being recognised as the 'Emperor of the Two Americas'. This dream did not run its expected course and was abandoned in favour of a French 'protectorate' over the whole of Portugal. Napoleon's army, although courteously received in Lisbon by the ruling class, soon outlived its welcome when Junot injudiciously flaunted the French flag and hectored the council of regency meeting in the old palace of the Inquisition. In the countryside hostility to the predatory behaviour of the invaders led to the growth of a guerrilla resistance and in Oporto a full-scale rebellion against foreign occupation broke out in June 1808. Two months later the future Duke of Wellington brought an expeditionary army from Ireland to Portugal which landed on the coast near Coimbra and rapidly defeated the French forces outside Lisbon. Junot, disappointed at not having been named king of Portugal, signed the Sintra peace convention with the British and the royal navy ferried the French army back home with all its weapons and booty intact. The generous terms of the surrender were blamed by slightly unfair public opinion on Wellington, then still plain Sir Arthur Wellesley, as shown in a fine contemporary satire:

> This is the City of Lisbon.
> This is the Gold that lay in the City of Lisbon.
> These are the French who took the Gold that lay in the City of Lisbon.
> This is Sir Arthur (whose Valour and Skill began so well, but ended so ill) who beat the French, who took the gold, that lay in the city of Lisbon.
> This is the *Convention* that Nobody owns, that saved old Junot's Baggage and Bones, altho' Sir Arthur (whose Valour and Skill began so well but ended so ill) had beaten the French who took the Gold that lay in the City of Lisbon.
> These are the Ships that carried the spoil that the French had plundered with so much toil after the Convention which nobody owns, that saved Old Junot's Baggage and Bones, although Sir Arthur (whose Valour and Skill began so well but ended so ill) had beaten the French who took the Gold that lay in the City of Lisbon.
> This is John Bull, in great dismay, at the sight of the ships which carried away the gold and silver and all the spoil, the French had plundered with so much toil, after the Convention which nobody owns, which saved old Junot's Baggage and Bones, altho' Sir Arthur (whose Valour and Skill began so well but ended so ill) had beaten the French who took the Gold that lay in the city of Lisbon.
> Cited and illustrated in José Hermano Saraiva, *História de Portugal* (1983–4, Lisbon) volume v, p. 133.

Capturing the Portuguese bullion reserves was not enough to satisfy Napoleon, and he embarked on further attempts at conquering Britain's surviving territory in continental Europe. To meet the new invasions Wellington, recovering from his ignominious 'victory convention' of 1808, was sent back to Portugal with new British troops and a cadre of officers to help train up a more effective Portuguese army than the one that had been brushed aside by Junot in his 1807 march on Lisbon. The second French invasion which captured Oporto in 1808 was driven out by the British troops. The new Portuguese army, drilled and disciplined by Viscount Beresford who was appointed its commander with the local rank of marshal,

24   At the battle of Bussaco (Buçaco) in 1810 the Portuguese
army, with British assistance, delayed the second attempt by
the French to capture Lisbon and caused their eventual failure
before 'the lines of Torres Vedras'.

had its baptism of fire at the battle of Bussaco where it fought alongside Wellington's troops in September 1810. In the battle a third
French invasion, consisting of 60,000 French troops under the command of General Massena, was temporarily waylaid on the road to
Lisbon, though the soldiers recovered enough comprehensively to
sack the city of Coimbra and continue their march southward. Some
miles further on the French encountered a maze of military trenches
and palisades at Torres Vedras which blocked the paths to Lisbon.
Building these lines of defence had cost Portuguese workers months
of forced labour on short rations when already the Peninsular Wars
were taking their toll in disease and malnutrition. To stop the French
from feeding themselves by scouring the countryside the British had
imposed a scorched earth policy of destroying food hoards and burning the sails of windmills to prevent corn milling. Eventually the
French, blocked by the palisades, drenched by the winter rains and
deprived of local rations, were compelled to retreat into Spain. They
took with them many unfortunate Portuguese conscripts forced to
fight on for five more years in defence of Napoleon's collapsing
empire. They also took with them much of Portugal's scarce stock

of horses, thus further undermining the Portuguese transport system as well as decimating the cavalry. The Peninsular Wars had been an inglorious time of suffering for nearly all the peoples of Portugal.

One of the most profound consequences of the Peninsular Wars was the flight of the Portuguese court of Maria I and the prince regent to Brazil in the winter of 1807 to 1808. This flight stimulated the Brazilian idea of a North-American-style independence movement. The long, slow shift of Brazil towards independence had been one of the fundamental features of the reign of Maria I. She had ascended the throne in 1777, only a year after the thirteen colonies in North America had declared their rebellion against Britain. The lucidity with which Thomas Jefferson and his American colleagues proclaimed the rights of man, and especially the freedoms of colonial citizens, had a significant impact on the literate white population of Brazil. By the time the old Portuguese queen died, in the year after Waterloo, American democracy had become entrenched, Europe had been through the French Revolution, Haiti had undergone the great bid for freedom by the black peoples of the Caribbean and Brazilian independence was only six years away.

The first signs of a Brazilian independence movement had occurred long before in the gold-rich province of Minas Gerais. As in the British and Spanish American colonies it was wealthy white settlers who wanted to eliminate the foreign apex of colonial society while at the same time retaining the rest of the hierarchy of order and privilege. Potential leaders of Brazil viewed the emergence of the United States and its republican form of government with favour and in 1786 they made discreet contact with Jefferson while he was the American envoy to France. Tacit United States approval encouraged a liberation conspiracy to develop among the richest men in Brazil with some support from the armed forces. The idea was legitimated by Brazilian scholars and jurists, and celebrated by philosophers and poets. The independence movement was also strong among exiles, and particularly among the 300 Brazilian students enrolled at Coimbra university. They travelled to France to read Voltaire and Rousseau, and to Britain where they encountered the theories of constitutional freedom expounded by John Locke, concepts which were banned in Portugal and its colonies. Subversive ideas were carried back to Brazil and the network of police informers later revealed that they had been discussed even in the remotest frontier districts of the interior. It was in Minas Gerais, however, that the first attempt at revolution occurred although it achieved little of the success gained by North Americans in Philadelphia.

The population of Minas Gerais at the time of the attempted revolution consisted of 300,000 colonists and an unknown number of indigenous Brazilian 'Indians'. Half the colonists were imported black slaves, predominantly male, and a quarter were white immigrants, also predominantly male, while the rest were locally-born creoles of various racial mixtures. The provincial economy had become widely diversified since the gradual decline of gold production in the 1760s, and some former mine owners had bought cattle ranches, pig farms, sugar plantations, rum distilleries and market gardens to feed the urban population. The search for gold continued but the easy alluvial deposits had been exhausted and the deep seams had to be expensively quarried. Mine magnates sought to reduce their costs by making the province self-sufficient not only in food but also in mining equipment. The Portuguese government remained sternly opposed to the 'liberal' idea that gold miners might smelt their own iron and forge their own tools but the interior nevertheless broke away from the mercantilist thraldom of empire which continued to hold the coastal plantations. Unlike any other province of Portuguese South America, Minas Gerais acquired local business leaders with the skills to bid against Lisbon entrepreneurs for the award of local tax-raising contracts. The taste for autonomy and for regional economic integration stimulated industrial captains to aspire to independence.

The leaders of Minas Gerais society mostly came from the north of Portugal rather than from Lisbon or the south and belonged to an integrated social culture which dominated the other racial strands. Educated immigrants possessed extensive libraries, met in philosophical debating clubs, translated the work of Adam Smith, and even erased their provincial Oporto origins by buying their way into the nobility. Lower-class whites commonly came from the Azores Islands in mid-Atlantic and cherished their distinct identity. Slaves, even those of the second and third generation, maintained strong cultural ties with African religion, music and dance and often brought to Brazil a sharp commercial acumen which served their owners well. Mestiços held most of the petty administrative jobs, although legislation frequently attempted to preserve such positions for whites. Since white wives were relatively rare, the sons of even the higher ranks of society were often brown rather than white but were nonetheless given a proper education and professional preferment. The religious orders were more strict than the state in their racial exclusion of persons with any evidence of mestiço, Jewish or heretical ancestry but nevertheless flourished and built exuberant rococo churches. The armed forces were even more punctilious in maintaining racial segregation, but all three estates were proud of the wealth, culture and distinctive identity of Minas Gerais society.

The objectives of the upper-class Brazilian conspirators who hoped to break away from the Portuguese crown in 1789 were predominantly economic and self-seeking despite the high-flown constitutional philosophy in which they were couched. They wanted restrictions on diamond prospecting to be lifted; they wanted the freedom to develop local industries, for instance by opening a gunpowder factory to meet their strategic needs; they wanted their own university, the cachet of cultural success in any new nation; they wanted a citizens' militia to replace the colonial army and they wanted child allowances for white women to increase the development of a loyal local population. Brazilian separatists went further and proposed sumptuary laws which would require even members of high society to restrict their wardrobes to clothes of local manufacture. Such economic nationalism, and talk of local democratic councils and of a parliamentary colonial government, frightened Portugal and caused the authorities to crush the rebellion and hang its leader, lieutenant Silva Xavier, the *Tiradentes* (the 'Teethscrewer'), in 1792 who had become a powerful figure of patriotic folklore. Soon afterwards the idea of white independence in Latin America received a severe setback with the outbreak of a black rebellion in Haiti. White aspirations in Brazil were postponed lest they open the floodgates of social revolution in communities where half the population was enslaved and many more suffered from racial disabilities. But the idea of black liberation, sharply contrasted to the mine owners' rebellion, did reach Brazil and a second independence movement broke out in the predominantly black northern city of Bahia.

The Bahia rebels of 1798 were led by mestiço artisans and crafts-men in much the fashion of the Haiti rebellion which had been initiated by semi-privileged, semi-white colonial subjects seeking to gain the advantages of revolution. While the Portuguese government had been persecuting the literary élites of Rio de Janeiro suspected of Jacobin tendencies because they read books published in Britain, real Jacobin ideas from France had been reaching the racially despised lower middle class in Bahia and encouraging concepts of fraternity and equality. The Bahia rebels were very different from the middle-aged white magistrates of Minas Gerais who had initially sought a break with Portugal. They were young soldiers, apprentices, share-croppers, wage-earners, school-teachers, and craftsmen. They were as much opposed to the Brazilian propertied classes, and to the op-pressive social order maintained by the church, as they were to their foreign political masters. They were led by a 'coloured' tailor who sought equality of opportunity, regardless of race, and aspired to a French pattern of democratic government. More dramatically still they spread leaflets around the city of Bahia demanding the liber-ation of the slaves. Such radicalism was crushed with even greater firmness than the upper-class rebellion of ten years earlier.

The mining rebellion of 1789 and the racial rebellion of 1798 shook colonial society so strongly that a compromise alliance be-tween the propertied class in Brazil and the ruling class in Portugal delayed Brazilian independence by nearly a generation. Some eco-nomic liberalisation was permitted, for instance in the salt industry, and Brazilians who had abandoned their French-style republicanism were given government positions. Recognition of the economic pri-macy of Brazil within the Lusitanian empire was confirmed when the court arrived in Rio de Janeiro in 1808. Political change fol-lowed without threatening the old social stability and Brazil eventu-ally enjoyed almost a century more of monarchical government and slave-owning prosperity. Diplomatically and commercially Brazil also maintained its close ties with Britain. The Rio de Janeiro royal court was compelled to sign the British treaty of 1810 which for-malised the opening of the ports of Brazil to direct shipping from Britain. This may have helped the British to evade French naval interference in the trade, but more significantly it allowed them to avoid the payment of commission to traditional Portuguese middlemen in Lisbon. The commercial independence of Brazil was followed twelve years later by political independence in 1822.

The *ancien régime* in Portugal came to an end in three steps which paralleled mainstream developments of European history. A revolt in 1820, modelled on the democratic Spanish revolution of 1812, led to the ending of the British occupation, the drafting of a democratic constitution and the reluctant recognition of Brazilian independence. Ten years later, following the European liberal revolutions of 1830, Portugal made a second attempt at fundamental political reform, expelled Miguel I, a royal pretender with absolutist aspirations, confiscated the crown lands and dissolved the monasteries. Finally in 1851, in the wake of the 1848 revolutions in Europe, a parliamentary regime was established after a period of technocratic dictatorship and a rather virulent peasant revolt. Thereafter Portugal once again embarked on a modest programme of industrialisation and was brought into closer contact with Europe by the railway age.

The Portuguese revolutionary movement which broke out in 1820 was concerned with much more than a patriotic restoration of independence after the foreign occupations. It was an expression of the growth of liberalism that had accompanied social and economic transformation throughout the reign of Maria I. In some respects Portugal had been more adaptable to change than some other countries of Latin Europe in the late eighteenth century and the queen's ministers had kept one step ahead of revolutionary pressures though the queen herself retreated into a world of pious fantasy. Members of the court who read Adam Smith and Montesquieu were far more enlightened than their Spanish counterparts and aired such novel ideas as proposals to tax the nobility and the clergy. Near-revolutionary suggestions to finance the state by selling crown and church lands to private buyers among the growing ranks of the bourgeoisie were already being debated before the French invasions. The royal bureaucracy had even prepared draft legislation on agricultural reform and industrial expansion before it fled to Brazil, though the crown failed to adopt such radical initiatives, fearing that it would alienate the aristocratic class on which it had come to depend rather more than in the days of Pombal. The more ardent reformers were temporarily optimistic that Junot and his French invaders might be more sympathetic to new forms of wealth creation, and to the liberalisation of social relations, than the members of the aristocracy who had sailed to Brazil with their British 'captors'.

The liberal precursors of the Portuguese Revolution welcomed the French to Portugal in 1807 with far-ranging expectations of new land tenure, new legal structures, an abolition of feudal privilege, a separation of church and state, equality of taxation, constitutional restraints on the monarchy and above all a restitution of the almost lost colonies. Industrialists in particular saw the French invasion as a golden opportunity to rid themselves of competition from British imports. The French invaders, however, showed little interest in supporting a social and economic reform programme advanced by industrialists and intellectuals. They were more concerned with strategic stability and sought their accomplices not among liberals but among those members of the nobility and clergy that had been left behind when the court sailed to Brazil. They failed to recognise the benefits France might have reaped from Portugal's strong anti-British feelings, and far from encouraging liberal collaborators they persecuted reformers. Liberal euphoria at the French arrival was soon replaced by disillusion. As a consequence when popular rebellion broke out in June 1808 the protests were couched in nationalist rather than revolutionary terms. The precursors of the Portuguese Revolution did not adopt revolutionary slogans or build a lasting alliance between town and country such as had given substance to the French Revolution, but clamoured instead for a return of the king and freedom from French occupation regardless of other ideological considerations.

In the failed revolution of 1808 the middle class was rapidly neutralised as the nobility recovered its old authority and the *ancien régime* carried on after only the smallest of hiccups. The church, after a momentary fright induced by the arrival of French free-thinkers, set about persecuting dissidents with its old indiscriminate prejudice. Any shame that members of the *ancien régime* had felt about collaborating with the French was expunged in a welter of repression directed at the threat of popular rebellion. The conservative power of the old order was further strengthened by the return of the British who postponed any serious attempt at renewed revolution by a decade. During those ten years, however, the Portuguese middle class gained renewed vigour as merchants recovered from the partial loss of the Brazil trade and benefited from contracts to supply the needs of the British army of occupation.

Many of the new industrial ventures that were to be so important to nineteenth-century Portugal were focused on the city of Oporto where some of the later revolutionary initiatives originated. One particularly successful industry was linen spinning and weaving. Flax was imported from Hamburg and farmed out to thousands of cottage artisans in the districts north of the city where population had reached saturation point and work was scarce. The success of the Oporto entrepreneurs was based on the avoidance of factory building costs and on the cheapness of village labour which was paid by the piece. When business was slack workers, both men and women, had to fall back on peasant subsistence and could expect none of the minimal security to which proletarian factory workers might aspire. When business flourished the cottage weavers became so skilled that their piece goods could match the linens of France and Holland and compete with English woollens in Brazil. Textile weaving became the base for other small industries as the profits of linen were invested in ways that were essentially new to Portugal. The industrial region round Oporto developed ironmongery, crockery, cutlery, buttons, barrels, ribbons baize and hats, though linen remained the key industry until challenged by the growth and mechanisation of cotton spinning.

The infant cotton textile industry of Portugal had enjoyed some advantage in the late eighteenth century. Raw cotton could still be obtained from Brazil and finished cotton materials were not subject to protected British competition in the same way that woollens were since cotton goods had not existed at the time of Methuen and so were not mentioned in his treaty of 1703. The main centre of the cotton industry was Lisbon rather than Oporto and, unlike the linen industry, production was based on factories using imported machinery from Britain. The great aspiration of all textile manufacturers in Portugal was an expanded access to the Brazilian market. The key issue of economic reform for the industrial bourgeoisie was therefore the restoration of imperial preference and the abolition of the trade treaty of 1810 which had ended the Methuen Treaty and

given all British manufactures direct access to Brazil. Such industrial aspiration was supported by the merchant class which had also
lost business through the new British treaty. Although wine traders
were not as tied to the colonial markets as textile traders, southern
wines sold more abundantly in Brazil than in Europe and Lisbon
vintners therefore supported the revolutionary demand that the
British be expelled and Brazil be restored to Portugal as a preferential
market.

   In nineteenth-century Portugal the towns, especially Lisbon and
Oporto, continued to dominate the political scene. Lisbon was still
one of the great cities of Europe, and most of Portugal's goldsmiths
and booksellers congregated there, supplying the needs of the almost exclusively urban professional class. The overall level of urbanisation had changed little from the days of the sixteenth-century
empire though Oporto, which had long remained a small market
town with streets full of pigs, continued to grow and doubled in size
between 1801 and 1864. The city's shops, offices and manufactories
remained in the old twisting city centre while rich colonial returnees
from Brazil built miniature palaces with ornamental iron balconies
in the eastern suburbs. English wine shippers and stockbrokers continued to own the elegant residences on the west side of the town.
The municipal councillors introduced gas lighting to emphasise the
status of their merchant city and the Oporto bourgeoisie emulated
foreigners by eating toast and drinking their tea with milk. Despite
the growth of Oporto the national index of urbanisation remained
low at 11 per cent. Even Spain, whose social structure was similar,
was more industrialised and urbanised than Portugal, and a hundred
years after the revolution 84 per cent of Portugal's population still
lived in villages. This lack of development was both the cause and
the consequence of continued overseas emigration. The tiny provincial towns provided few opportunities for education, employment
or emancipation from rural drudgery and so the old tradition of emigration took on a new momentum in the nineteenth century. Many
successful emigrants did not choose to return and when they did so
were mocked as uncouth *nouveaux riches*. Less successful migrants
could not afford to buy a passage home or face the expectations
of their relations. Since Portugal's twin cities did not attract many
of the dynamic and ambitious youths who were fleeing from rural

stagnation with their eyes set on Brazil and the United States, the search for social and political change was left in the hands of a rather cautious bourgeoisie and a few imaginative aristocratic soldiers.

The first military hero of the Portuguese Revolution was a martyr who was already dead by the time of the 1820 uprising. Gomes Freire had been a cosmopolitan army officer who had been born in Vienna and had served in Napoleon's Portuguese legion. During the French occupation of Germany he rose to become governor of Dresden and received an honorary degree from the university of Jena. After the restoration of the *ancien régime* he returned to Portugal to be politically rehabilitated. In Lisbon he became grandmaster of the Portuguese freemasons, a movement which had spread widely among army officers who had fraternised with both French and British masons during the periods of foreign occupation. The Portuguese masonic lodges were to play a significant political role during and after the revolutionary years, much to the consternation of the ecclesiastical authorities. Between 1810 and 1820 the masonic grandmaster became a heroic patriot noted for his liberal views, for his opposition to the return of an absolutist monarchy, for his criticism of the council of regency and above all for his hostility to Marshal Beresford, the British commander-in-chief of the Portuguese army. When rumours of a plot to overthrow the government and expel the British spread through Lisbon in 1817 Gomes Freire was arrested and convicted of treason. His status as Portugal's national hero was greatly enhanced and blame for his conviction was placed on Beresford. Far from quelling the rise of national restiveness the execution was interpreted by the Lisbon crowd as martyrdom and it accelerated the move towards rebellion against the British occupation.

The Portuguese Revolution broke out in earnest on 24 August 1820 in Oporto. Eighty city merchants and a couple of aristocrats 'pronounced' against the British occupation while Beresford was safely out of the country visiting the king in Brazil and seeking an extension of his almost viceregal authority. On 15 September the revolution spread to Lisbon but in a more radical guise with frustrated soldiers taking the lead and merchants recognising that they could not resist the popular clamour. Leaders from the two cities met at Coimbra to formulate a moderate agenda asking for the expulsion of the British, the restoration of the monarchy and the re-establishment of the Brazil trade. None of these objectives were fully attained but politics took on a new lease of life after ten years of quiescence. The rebels were able to organise the election of a constituent assembly to plan constitutional structures for a new Portugal. The delegates, when elected, turned out somewhat surprisingly to belong to the professional rather than the commercial middle class. There were twenty university lecturers but only three merchants, forty lawyers but only two proprietors, fourteen priests but no abbots. Strikingly there were no representatives of the colonial interests, the wine trade or industry, and less surprisingly there were no plebeian representatives of the people who were the supposed heroes of the revolution. The new politicians were predominantly liberal graduates of Pombal's reformed university.

The constitution makers of 1820 began their task with cautious modesty but in their debates did not shun the conflicts and difficulties which they faced. They wanted the royal family to return from Brazil, though they came to the opinion that the nation was sovereign and that the Braganzas should be elected to the throne and that their veto should only be allowed to delay legislation, not suppress it. They wanted Catholicism to be the normal religion of Portugal, but would not accept that it should be the sole religion and when the cardinal patriarch protested at the entrenchment of religious toleration he was driven into exile in France. They objected to legal privileges for the clergy but left inequalities in lay society untouched. They wanted civic rights to be broadened, but they also wanted to protect property ownership which so severely divided the class from which they came from the poor who served them. They were happy to abolish feudal controls over olive oil presses, herb pharmacies and communal ovens in the countryside but were reluctant to reform social relations in the towns. They wanted a parliament but devoted heated debates to the merits of a single parliamentary chamber, favoured by radicals, democrats and republicans, as against a two-chamber parliament favoured by monarchists, conservatives and Catholics. They saw themselves as democrats but some of them had begun political life in Oporto as members of a secret society committed to subverting the *ancien régime*. They were political theorists rather than practised politicians and they were

25 On the plain of Alentejo, south of the River Tagus, southern villagers have used communal ovens to bake wheaten loaves
for centuries.

certainly not demagogues who expected to court votes among the
unlettered majority.

The political debates of the early revolution eventually culminated
in the adoption of the surprisingly radical constitution of 1822. This
was based on a constitution which had been drawn up at Cadiz in
1812 for adoption by Spain after the expulsion of the invaders of the
Peninsular Wars. Ten years later the democratic tenor of the doc-
ument was not to the liking of the conservative powers of restoration Europe. It was, however, tolerable to Britain even though the
proposed parliament had no hereditary upper chamber to curtail
the potential radicalism of elected deputies. The franchise was sufficiently liberal to permit the election of a parliament that would

contemplate legislative change to match the social change which
Portugal had been undergoing. Where the founding fathers of liberalism had failed to come to terms with their indecision was in regard
to the army. They did not approve of the military domination of politics which had persisted during the ten years of British control, but
they were not wholly adverse to seeking military support for their
own favourite causes or to calling on the army to curtail any move
that might go beyond their own cautious brand of radicalism. The
army became one of the key factors in the politics of revolution, and
in 1823 it was the army which turned out the first parliamentarians
who attempted to give a new face to national politics.

Before the army coup of 1823 a fundamental change had taken
place in the relations between Portugal and Brazil which was to affect the whole revolution. The former prince regent, now King John
VI, returned from Rio de Janeiro to Lisbon in 1821 to resume the
royal responsibilities he had abandoned in 1807. He left the affairs
of Brazil in the hands of his son Pedro saying, according to improbable local mythology, that if there was to be a Brazilian declaration
of independence he would rather his son should lead it and not
some unknown political opportunist. The expected declaration of
independence soon followed and Prince Pedro of Portugal became
Pedro I, emperor of Brazil. The declaration put in jeopardy the key
aspirations of the Portuguese Revolution and seriously undermined
the credibility of the parliamentarians who were striving to create
a new order based on the restoration of the empire. But although
Brazilian independence undermined the first steps towards democracy, the immediate occasion for the overthrow of parliamentary
government came not from Brazil but from Europe.

In 1823 France, under its restored and ultra-conservative Bourbon dynasty, invaded Spain to repress the supporters of the democratic constitution of Cadiz. The Cadiz constitution was the model
that had been adopted by the Portuguese constitutionalists of 1822
and it became their article of faith throughout the revolutionary
years. Portuguese moderates, on the other hand, feared that the
constitution might prove provocative to conservative Europe and
that the Holy Alliance might follow up the attack on Spain with
an invasion of Portugal to enforce a restoration of royal absolutism
in Lisbon. To avoid such an invasion, or worse still a civil war, a

Le maréchal-duc de Sal-lanah, nouvel ambassadeur de Portugal à Paris.

26   Field Marshal Saldanha was a leading military figure of the
Portuguese Revolution of 1820–51, and as a duke continued to
dominate the parliamentary and extra-parliamentary politics
of the constitutional monarchy until his death in 1876.

dashing young brigadier called Saldanha raised a small army and rode into Lisbon to abolish parliament and drive out the constitutional 'extremists'. The brigadier was a grandson of the Marquis of Pombal, the eighteenth-century dictator, and his coup was the first of several which he led over the next fifty years. To prevent the restoration of absolutism, and avoid the challenge of liberalism, Saldanha proposed a constitutional compromise in which the powers of the crown would be partially restored to the conciliatory King John VI. This moderate royalist *coup d'état* dismayed the conservatives who saw Saldanha as a subversive freemason, and scandalised the radicals who thought the king little better than a puppet when they discovered that he had recalled Beresford from Britain to be his most intimate adviser. Saldanha's coup put an end to the first phase of the Portuguese Revolution and signalled its failure to achieve its two central aims, the removal of British influence over Portuguese politics and the restoration of colonial power over Brazil. Worse still his promise of moderate royal paternalism was soon undermined by the king's death in 1826. The country steeled itself for the second stage of the revolution.

Liberal democracy, based on male literate suffrage, would probably not have long survived the challenge of the conservative forces which opposed the revolution. Its failure, however, was made virtually certain by the Brazilian declaration of independence in 1822. The commercial bourgeoisie which might have supported the parliamentarians had they recovered economic control over Brazil, turned against them when they lost control over the colony altogether. When John VI died in 1826 the country was split between radicals and absolutists and even the royal family was divided. Pedro, now emperor of Brazil, supported the claims of his infant daughter Maria and sought an accommodation with the radicals, while the dowager queen, and her young son Miguel, supported the restoration of absolutism. Pedro proposed a compromise constitutional 'charter' modelled on the French constitution. The charter would have given the crown authority to moderate between the legislative, executive and judicial powers of the state and would have introduced a house of lords with seventy-two aristocrats and nineteen bishops. Extremists on both sides criticised the proposal and the country slid towards civil war. British Tories, guided by Wellington

and Beresford, thought in vain that they could bring the two sides together and restore some British influence over Portugal. Wellington
dispatched Prince Miguel to Portugal after five years of exile in the
hope that he would become a constitutional regent on behalf of his
seven-year-old niece, Queen Maria II. Instead Miguel claimed the
crown for himself, driving thousands of liberals into exile in their
turn, and arousing patriotic support for his despotic political pretensions. Pedro thereupon abdicated the Brazilian throne and sailed
to Europe to fight for his daughter's heritage as queen of Portugal.
He gained support from France, which had turned to liberalism
in the revolution of 1830, and from Britain, which had turned the
old Duke of Wellington out of office and elected a liberal government whose foreign policy was dominated by Lord Palmerston. Both
countries gave military support to Pedro and the exiles when the
Portuguese civil war began in 1832.

The civil war of 1832 to 1834 marked a brutal mid-point in the
slowly developing revolution which carried Portugal from royal
absolutism to constitutional democracy. The war bitterly pitted the
two brothers Pedro and Miguel against each other. Miguel held
Lisbon and was encouraged by Austria to preserve the purity of his
royal prerogatives. He did so by instituting a reign of terror which
filled the prisons with liberal sympathisers and led to many deaths
from deprivation and persecution. Pedro, whose small liberal army
was based on the Azores Islands, landed at Oporto with the backing
of an Anglo-French mercenary force. He was supported not only by
the cream of the Portuguese intelligentsia but also by two young military leaders with political ambitions, Saldanha and Sá da Bandeira,
who were to become the heroes of the civil war and each of whom
was later to serve no fewer than five terms as prime minister.

The liberal crusade began slowly and Pedro's forces spent the first
year of the war besieged in Oporto. Although his officers could
dine in style with the English wine merchants his men suffered
from hunger and were decimated by cholera. The tide only turned
when Admiral Napier, the British commander of the liberal fleet,
destroyed the royalist fleet off the south coast and landed a force
which approached Lisbon from the south. The Lisbon mob then
rose up against the royalists who had dominated the city for five
years, expelled Miguel's garrison, captured the royal arsenal and

distributed weapons to the freed political prisoners. Pedro moved his headquarters to Lisbon while Miguel once again went into exile. After two years of bitter and destructive war Portugal was again bankrupt and beholden to its foreign creditors. The politicians, anxious lest Miguel return yet again with Austrian support and doubtful of the depth of Pedro's commitment to liberalism, adopted a radical agenda of social reconstruction that was to prove far-reaching and irreversible.

The ground cause of the radicalism of 1834 was the continued survival in Portugal of feudal-type institutions which bore harshly on the poor and had scarcely been reformed during the first phase of the revolution. The weight of customary extractions was illustrated by one farm near Lisbon owned by the royal family. It produced sixty measures of corn per year of which only twelve were retained by the farmer while thirty measures went to the landlord, six were charged for the porterage of tribute, five went in church tithes and the balance was levied as various state taxes. Other peasants paid a threshing tax, plough and oxen rentals, a milling fee and a cartage surcharge which could only be waived if all produce was delivered to a navigable riverbank by the farmer. To add to the strength of grievance peasants had no scales of their own and had to accept the bailiff's weights and measures, however false they might be. Widows received a particularly small share of their earnings and gained no compassionate remission of their ecclesiastical dues. One large priory controlled the revenues of twenty-nine parishes containing 6,000 homesteads and monopolised all the mills, presses, river boats and granaries of the district. The church spoils included one-tenth of all olive oil, an eighth of the linen, first-born livestock, and duty on bread, wine and fruit. Church revenues were used to feed the convents and rectories as well as pay the salaries of bishops. It was not surprising that the renewed fervour of the revolution in 1834 had strong anti-clerical overtones.

The radicalism of 1834 was partly due to a virulence of retribution against property owners and ecclesiastical institutions that had supported Miguel in his abolition of constitutional rule. The crown lands, amounting to one-quarter of the national territory, were taken over by the state to help pay the national debt either by the appropriation of revenues or by outright sale of land to private buyers.

Over 300 male monastic orders, most of them small but some of them possessing rich estates, were abolished and their lands sold to supporters of the liberal cause. This dissolution of the monasteries, like the dissolutions in sixteenth-century England, enriched a new class of rising landowners who were committed to the transfer of property and could not contemplate turning back to the *ancien régime*. The middle class, which had grown in influence under Maria I before the revolution, now gained more lands, more influence and more noble titles, under the child-queen Maria II. The confiscation of church lands was accepted in a wave of popular revulsion at the excessive clericalism of Miguel's supporters. The church properties that were redistributed were probably comparable in scale to those of the crown and were expected to pay off the liberal debts incurred during the civil war.

The sale of church and crown lands did not revitalise Portugal in the way that had been anticipated. The value of the lands sold fell as the supply exceeded the demand. With cheap plentiful land the new landowners decided perfectly rationally to continue the extensive and extractive farming practices of the past rather than investing scarce capital in the intensive new methods used elsewhere in Europe where land was scarce and valuable. Hoe farming or tilling by hand-drawn wooden ploughs was not replaced by deep ox-ploughing and soils were not harrowed and manured. Market forces did not lead to the breakup of the large, inefficient, latifundia estates of the south as was happening in other parts of the Mediterranean world. Labourers were so ill-paid that they continued to seek ways of escaping to Brazil. Two-thirds of the country remained semi-deserted, covered by unexploited wood, heath, marsh and arid mountain waste. Much of the land that was cultivated was still devoted to rudimentary peasant subsistence. In towns the confiscated ecclesiastical buildings were not turned into new schools or given over to other productive uses, as recommended by Henry VIII of England, but were handed to the army as luxurious residential barracks for soldiers in the manner favoured by Napoleon's coarse revolútionary troops. Within two years the idealism of the 'victors' in the civil war had run into the sand.

The revitalisation of the revolutionary momentum occurred in September 1836 and began with an urban uprising and a military *coup d'état*. The underlying cause of the uprising was chronic unemployment. One hundred thousand men had been under arms during the civil war and now had to be demobilised and integrated into the weak economy. Emigration was not an available solution for many and expectations of jobs at home were high. Shirtless peasants drifted to the city and Lisbon protested at the apathy of the royally approved government. The National Guard, far from quelling the uprising, sided with the protesters and approved the call for Sá da Bandeira to lead the nation and bring back the constitution of 1822. The city council summoned Queen Maria from her suburban palace to swear allegiance to the constitution. She looked, it was said, as affronted as Marie Antoinette had done when facing the guillotine. Some of the new propertied class were equally dismayed at the prospect of Lisbon mob rule or radical rule by the hero of the Oporto siege. The cautious franchise of the 1826 charter had given landowners all the authority that they sought and they were happy to ally themselves to the royal house. Their pragmatic leader, however, was the other great military hero of the liberal cause, Saldanha, and he was not willing to risk further bloodshed or a rekindling of the civil war in his attempts to upset the 'September' government. He therefore agreed the terms of a non-revolutionary reform programme with his old military associate, Sá da Bandeira, and a modest programme of modernisation could begin.

The pressure for renewed change came from the cities and from the merchant class who put the September ideology into practice with a series of social reforms. Not only was primary education reformed but grammar schools were established to replace the church schools that had been abolished. Commercial and industrial training was developed and academies of fine arts and drama were established. Polytechnics were created in both Lisbon and Oporto and even the university at Coimbra was mildly modernised again. Libraries were founded to receive the books of the dissolved monasteries and museums received their works of art. Civil registers of births, marriages and deaths were established to replace the ecclesiastical ones. The young queen was married into the great royal house of Saxe-Coburg, which already ruled Belgium and was soon to rule Britain as well. A German king-consort, the future Fernando II, came to Lisbon to guide her discreetly, and against her own conservative instincts, through the constitutional minefield which separated the purists of the constitution of 1822 who wanted power to be restored to the people and the legitimists of the charter of 1826 who thought power could only be conceded by benevolence of the crown. The virulence of the post-war settlement of old scores abated, though not before 1,000 political assassinations had been committed. Eventually a compromise between radicals and conservatives was achieved which brought nearly ten years of stability before the last phase of the revolution broke out in 1846.

The great hero of moderation in Portugal's September reforms of 1836 remained Sá da Bandeira. He had been born into a landed family near Lisbon in 1795 and as a youth took up the army as a career. In the Peninsular Wars he was wounded, taken prisoner and abandoned for dead after the loss of an amputated arm. Despite his physical handicap he remained a distinguished horseman, soldier and military engineer. He studied in Coimbra, Paris and London and became one of the most cosmopolitan members of Portugal's rising new aristocracy. He spent his exile during Miguel's usurpation in Spain, England and Brazil before landing at Oporto in 1832 to command the garrison during the civil war siege. During the war he kept a diary and afterwards wrote prolifically on political, economic, military and colonial matters. He remained fairly consistently on the liberal left and was the ideal figurehead to lead the protest against the creeping conservatism that had restricted the franchise in the election of 1836 and triggered off a renewed military intervention in politics. Sá da Bandeira's greatest ambition, however, was to restore the fortunes of Portugal by the renewal of its imperial destiny. In this he looked to Africa. He introduced legislation to outlaw the trade in slaves from Africa to Brazil. His purpose was to invest African labour in the creation of a new empire in Africa itself rather than transplant it to the now independent territories of Brazil. This dream of a third empire was to be a recurring one in each generation of Portuguese politics but its implementation had to be deferred for a hundred years. Only in the 1930s was the vision which Sá da Bandeira had had in the 1830s for colonising Angola and Mozambique effectively put into practice. In the meantime, however, a different programme of economic transformation and modernisation was adopted by the September-style governments. This policy looked to

Europe rather than to Africa and was led by a new generation of technocrats who came to the fore in Portuguese public life.

The new technocratic leader who gradually emerged after 1836 was Costa Cabral, governor of Lisbon and a confidant of the queen. He entered the government as minister for justice and devoted his talents to expunging the populist element from government policy, restoring diplomatic relations with the Vatican, and bringing back the conservative constitutional charter of 1826, to the delight of the queen whose father had drawn it up. The Cabral government, whose brisk leader reminded some of the Pombal style of administration, built its base on urban and commercial interests. It moved away from the old September leaders who were increasingly linked to the landowners and wanted protective tariffs for the wheat and wine they were growing on the lands they had acquired from the crown and the church. These tariffs introduced by the old liberal guard kept farm prices high, but encouraged contraband wheat from Spain and made food dear in the city. Cabral's policy favoured importing cheaper food for the 'proletarians' working for his new industrialists and reducing the trade restrictions which limited the activities of his merchant supporters. The old Pombal system of granting sharehold-ers of private companies monopolies in such traditional activities as tobacco processing, soap manufacturing and gunpowder grinding was re-established. The opposition complained about the preferen-tial, not to say fraudulent, granting of licences to profiteers and protested that parliament had come to resemble an auction room or a stock exchange. Before the speculative bubble could burst with a recession of world trade the modernisers were challenged from rural Portugal.

The increasingly right-wing technocrats who were claiming the liberal inheritance had been encouraging the new landowners to make better use of their lands and to turn old convent estates into productive manor house farms. Costa Cabral himself established a country seat at Tomar, one of Portugal's most famous castles, and lavishly landscaped the grounds. The key to rural develop-ment, as ever, was improved transport and the technocrats sought finance capital to build roads through a privatised public works com-pany. To attract foreign investors they had to offer stability rather than freedom. Authoritarian public services, rather than democratic processes, became a lasting feature of Portuguese society. The bureaucratisation and professionalisation of administration deeply affected people's attitudes to government and instilled a new subservience to clerks and engineers in place of the old feudal subservience to abbots and barons. To finance the new order the inland revenue was restructured and regional administrations were established under central control. Cabral was denounced by politicians of both left and right for simultaneously betraying the revolution and the counter-revolution. In 1846 a rebellion broke out in the third great civil confrontation of the Portuguese Revolution. This time the restiveness came neither from the middle-class radicals of Oporto nor from the city mob in Lisbon but from the remote peasants in the northern province of Minho.

The north of Portugal was a world far removed from the politics of the capital city. Traditionally the hill farmers of the Minho grew wheat in the alluvial valleys and millet or rye on the more rugged ground. During fallow years, when their soil was recovering its fertility, they grazed livestock or cut hay on the alternating strips of farmland. Hilltops were used to pasture animals brought up from the village and to gather wild nuts from the old stands of chestnut which survived from Roman times. The settlement pattern was of the Germanic style with cultivators living on their scattered plots rather than in nucleated settlements. Housing was a simple combination of barn, stall, kitchen and shelter. Communities of half a dozen families worked three or four hectares each and an average holding might produce fifty bushels of wheat, thirty of rye, ten of millet and maintain four cows. Family labour was used to plant cereals in the autumn and flax in the spring. Calves for the Oporto slaughterhouse provided a cash supplement to the subsistence economy. Milk was a major beverage and wine only came to the highlands on feast days. Pigs were raised on acorns and salted down for the winter. In the woods small game was hunted and chestnuts were foraged both to feed animals and for human consumption in lean years. Cabbage soup was the regular daily fare but no olive oil came up the mountain to season it. Fruit was also rare since all imports had to be bought from muleteers. Women wove their own skirts and men wore straw overcoats like thatch to keep off the rain. The most prestigious purchase from the plain was gold to make personal ornaments to be worn at festivals. Mountain women wore pendants, necklaces, rings and filigree hearts to demonstrate their status in peasant society.

By the eighteenth century a slow agricultural revolution had penetrated the Minho with the introduction of Brazilian maize as a new crop. It first replaced the hardier cereals but in time was found to yield twice as much as wheat and so took over the fertile valleys as well. Maize farming required more work than the old pattern but manuring yielded good harvests and enabled more land to be brought into production than hitherto. Rising prosperity led to the building of new barns for drying and storing the greater harvest. Peasants became wealthier and more anxious to protect their homes and harvests, especially when the troubles of the French and British invasions began in 1807. What had been marginal backlands became productive farmlands and began to attract interest from people in the small towns who had previously neglected subsistence farms. Land users became landowners and the buying, selling and renting of land became an attractive proposition. The new agricultural productivity brought about by the maize revolution was further enhanced by the introduction of the American potato. In 1845, however, the potato crop failed in Portugal as elsewhere and brought bitter distress. The famine was made worse by the fact that better nutrition had been leading to rising human fertility and an increase in family size. It was in this bursting northern community that the third and last phase of the Portuguese Revolution broke out in 1846.

The most striking aspect of the northern rebellion of 1846 was the leading role played in it by women. The economic importance and the legal autonomy of women in the north of Portugal was an unusual feature of the local society. As land had become scarce plots were divided and subdivided until they were inadequate to maintain a family. Intensive agriculture became increasingly dependent on women while men were driven to emigrate, either temporarily or permanently. Although absentee men in the Americas did send cash remittances to their mothers and wives, women bore the brunt of family and farm management. Women became heads of household and owners of land. It was they who felt threatened by the bureaucratic intrusion of government under the Cabral regime of the early 1840s. A vanguard of women led the rebellion of the north and the movement was given the name Maria da Fonte. This 'Mary by the Fountain' came to resemble the mythical 'Captain Swing' of rebel folklore among English farmers.

The main trigger to the rebellion of 1846 was an attempt to enclose land and register its ownership. Land registry offices were set up which enabled literate, prosperous, middle-class land purchasers to register their titles in defiance of local custom. Traditional land users with no education and no access to lawyers had no means of countering the claims of the new gentry. Lands which were used for occasional foraging, for communal grazing, for charcoal burning, for trapping and snaring, were converted into private property patrolled by the aggressive bailiffs and gamekeepers of the new owners. The informal sector of the rural economy which had provided the margin between survival and emigration was eroded. Peasant protest at the loss of traditional rights to glean the fields or collect fuel in the woods was specific and angry. Far from being religious fanatics the Maria da Fonte rebels were highly rational local leaders who aspired to burn down the new land registry offices.

The rebels of 1846 were able to play skilfully on local anxieties. They accurately recognised that the modernising regime of Costa Cabral wanted to perfect a land tax system to finance its grandiose public works projects. Each landholder was expected to find a literate person who would fill in for them a bureaucratic form revealing their financial interests. Such an intrusion into conservative peasant privacy by untrustworthy city lawyers fuelled northern anger. The leaders of the rebellion gained further support by claiming, largely falsely, that the registration of land was being undertaken so that government could sell the enclosed farm strips to those great bogeymen of northern Portugal, the English. The English were the ethnically distinct and harshly exploitative suppliers of all the material goods and luxury wares which every peasant aspired to possess but which few could afford. The English were arrogant creditors who foreclosed on defaulting customers and took away their land. They represented everything that was most harsh and exploitative and aroused fervent nationalist sentiments among their rural customers. These national sentiments led the Maria da Fonte women to remember the exiled Prince Miguel and proclaim him as their national saviour. His reign of terror in Lisbon was ignored or forgotten

27 The peasant uprising in 1846 which brought the last phase of the civil war in the Portuguese Revolution was led in part by women who feared the loss of their land rights.

and the ideal of a pure royalist patriot gained wide appeal, spreading the rebellion and frightening the government. To make matters worse the rebels made common cause with the church which was seeking to regain the authority it had lost in the monastic dissolutions of 1834.

One of the most tendentious innovations by Costa Cabral's brisk regime of radical right-wing reformers was its public health legislation. It announced that burials should in future take place in cemeteries outside of the towns in contravention of Portuguese mourning customs. Traditionally the proper care of the dead involved placing the bodies in charnel houses inside churches until the bones could be retrieved and given a respected resting place in family vaults. The women were outraged at the outlawing of such pious customs and formed an alliance of protest with their priests. When government officials tried to interfere with funerals they were attacked and the coffins of the dead were taken back into the churches and defended by armed bands. The rebels were encouraged by a similar outcry across the border in Spain where the government had also interfered with burial customs and unleashed a peasant revolution. Religion had been restored to the political agenda after the early anti-clericalism of the revolution. The discomfiture of the Costa Cabral government increased when protest spread from the countryside to the town. There the government was attacked by the educated classes for abolishing the hard-won freedom of the press. In the crisis civil liberties were curtailed and martial law declared. Soldiers refused to fire on their kith and kin but deserted to join dissidents in the north in forming a revolutionary government in Oporto. Costa Cabral fell and his reform movement came to a temporary halt while a government of national reconciliation was put together in Lisbon to deal with the country's creditors.

The national politicians who sought to take over the government from Costa Cabral were not interested in the radical demands of the rebels. They belonged to the middle class and were fearful of egalitarian principles and millenarian fervour. They opposed rural demands that toll roads be abolished and peasants be allowed to use their old cart tracks free of charge. They certainly did not want a country dominated by a national guard of volunteers who elected their own officers from the ranks. They were in favour of the growth of capitalism and the spread of market values for land. The merchants among them had actually benefited from rising profits during the food crisis and potato failure that had accentuated the virulence of the northern rebellion. But hunger and the national financial crisis brought panic to Lisbon and Saldanha, the trouble-shooter and self-appointed saviour of Portugal, once again took charge of government. His coup, however, was unacceptable to the burghers of Oporto and triggered off a minor civil war within the framework of the revolution.

After the end of the first civil war in 1836 the centre of gravity of Portugal shifted with the decline of Oporto and the further rise in economic importance of Lisbon. Industrial growth was in Lisbon, the money market was in Lisbon and Lisbon politicians gave protection to their commercial associates. In 1846 the autumn revolt of Oporto, unlike the spring revolt of the Minho, was led by frustrated modernisers who approved of the Costa Cabral ideology but were dismayed that their own share of trade and industry was on the wane. The rebels chose as their leader Sá da Bandeira, the old ideologue of September and the great rival of Saldanha. But Sá da Bandeira remained a shrewd compromiser and feared that leading an Oporto army in an attack on the capital at a time of famine in the city might unleash the old radicalism which he had so carefully curtailed ten years before. Instead of fanning the flames of civil war he entered into negotiations with Britain, where Costa Cabral had fled into exile, and settled terms for his return to take responsibility for the national debt. The briefly discredited leader was thus restored to power in 1848 and ruled for another three years. In 1851, however, he was once again evicted from office, once again by Saldanha. This time the former brigadier, now a duke, appointed himself prime minister and ruled reasonably progressively from the house of lords for a full five-year term of office. His oligarchic democracy adopted the slogan 'regeneration' and brought twenty years of stability to Portugal.

Saldanha's military coup of 1851 brought the Portuguese Revolution to an end. In many respects the revolutionary era had been an unstable one. In thirty-one years there had been forty governments in which a limited number of army officers, intellectuals and aristocrats had served in the magic roundabout of ministerial posts. The revolutionary years had nonetheless brought lasting change. The new middle class had gained from the sale of national lands and was rapidly accumulating titles of nobility and becoming a steadily more conservative political influence. Commerce continued to be influenced by British custom, and even by British weights and measures. Politicians eventually adopted the British ideal of having two narrowly distinguished political parties and a two-chamber parliament. The educated class tended to be more deeply imbued with French ideas, and the bureaucracy created extensive French-style employment in a greatly extended system of both central and provincial administration. More surprisingly the élite also gained its foreign ideologies and customs from Spain. Because of the traditional inter-state hostility Portuguese historiography has tended to underestimate the influence of Spain on Portuguese political thinking and yet each stage of the revolution could be seen to mirror developments in Spain. Influential factions of the royal family continued to be members of the Spanish aristocracy whose loyalty to Portugal was often potentially suspect. On the other side of the political spectrum Portuguese radicals could easily read the publications of their Spanish contemporaries and be influenced by them. By the end of the revolution, however, the dominant influence on the whole generation of politicians had been the 'chartists'. They were the moderate royalists who came back from Brazil to confront both the quasi-republican constitutionalists of 1822 who admired Spanish radicalism, and the intransigent absolutists of 1828 who were guided by the opposite extremism espoused by the Spanish dowager queen.

When Saldanha seized power in 1851 he epitomised a dynamic tradition of aristocratic military politicians. He tended to belong to the liberal right but his exact loyalties fluctuated in the search for a middle course. His understanding of the economic interests that underlay the revolution had probably been rather weak. The basic debate, in so far as it was openly expressed in theoretical rather than personality terms, was one between free traders and protectionists. The free traders among the 1820 liberals were by and large merchants whose interests coincided with the British trade which they did not want to hinder. French-style economic nationalism was more robustly defended by farming and manufacturing interests which wanted tariff protection against imports. Protectionism was also

28   The 'Victorian' middle class of Lisbon dressed in elegant
French fashions and promenaded down avenues of French-style
architecture.

the policy of the September liberals but as they gave way to the
Cabral modernisers free trade was again adopted and even the pref-
erences granted to Portuguese shipping were abolished in an effort
to enhance the overall volume of trade and improve the profits of
traders. The regime of 1851 turned back to selective protectionism
with a renewed ambition to limit British economic domination and
protect production behind a tariff wall. The new, democratic Portugal entered the Age of Regeneration, though with an old-fashioned
cavalry officer at the helm.

5

The bourgeois monarchy and the republicans

The democratic era of regeneration that began in Portugal in 1851 created a two-party system of government which sought to modernise the country in line with the economic development being undertaken in many other small European kingdoms of the 'Victorian' age. The process was interrupted at several turning points. In 1870 an economic recession descended on Europe which undermined the basis of such prosperity as Portugal had achieved by reducing the price of wine and restricting the opportunities to export it. This very temporary recession mildly stimulated the manufacture of import substitutes and once again launched the debate on industrialisation policy. It also encouraged politicians to think again about colonial opportunities. A grandiose plan emerged for a new empire in Africa linking the old slaving ports of the east and west coasts with a 'rose-coloured map' spanning the continent. This imperial ambition was eroded first by Belgium and then by an ultimatum from Britain ordering Portugal to withdraw from the Zambezi heartland. Portugal had to settle reluctantly for more modest claims in Angola and Mozambique. The colonial question brought about a crisis of confidence in the crown which led to republican riots. Republicanism gained ground in the 1890s when the rising urban proletariat suffered from genuine deprivation during a prolonged economic recession. At the same time political awareness was increasing in the armed forces and junior officers organised themselves in secret cells of 'carbonari' to rival the cells of freemasons among senior officers. In 1908 republican extremism led to the assassination of King

Carlos followed two years later by the expulsion of his young son and the declaration of a Portuguese republic. The intelligentsia took over political command of the nation but new initiatives were soon undermined by the outbreak of the First World War. In 1917 Britain pressurised its 'oldest ally' to declare war on Germany and Portugal was rapidly bankrupted and demoralised. It briefly but abortively tried to solve its problems with a brisk military-style dictatorship before republican civilians began the long post-war task of reconstruction. The efforts of the democrats were constantly undermined, however, by a subversive opposition which eventually engendered a *coup d'état* by Catholic army officers in 1926. By 1930 the soldiers had surrendered power to a technocratic dictatorship which had to confront the great world depression and the closing of Brazil to all Portuguese transactions of trade, finance and migration. The monetarist autocrat who took charge of the government, António Salazar, modelled some of his ideas on Italian fascism and survived in office for forty austere years.

The attempts by mid-nineteenth-century democratic royalists to create a modern state with adequate systems of transport and education should not disguise the fact that to the majority of Portuguese social reality remained a peasant struggle for subsistence and survival. The northern peasants had aired their grievances in the uprising of 1846 which temporarily clipped the wings of predatory modernisers spreading out from the city. In the south the peasant way of life was less directly influenced by government, either for better or for worse. Nineteenth-century southern society used a technology largely inherited from the Muslim period to grow wheat, oats, rye, barley, olives and wine, and to raise sheep, goats, cattle, horses and pigs. Rich estate owners preferred to eat wheaten loaves while their workers were given rye bread as their portion. When late in the century protective tariffs made it economically rational to introduce steam threshing machines in place of flailing and winnowing, the machine operators were paid in wheaten bread to emphasise their status but landowners held out against the spread of wheat rations to ordinary workers.

Under the liberal ascendancy southern land tenure was slowly modified when monastic and royal land was auctioned off and 'feudal' restrictions on land purchase, consolidation or inheritance were

29   Medal struck for the Lisbon Agricultural Exhibition of 1884.

removed in favour of the self-made men of the bourgeois monarchy. Successful landowners already possessing hundreds of acres began to encroach on 'communal' lands which had been granted by the royal family to municipal trustees to enable common folk to graze stock and sow crops. Some of these strips were enclosed, and even sold, but peasants felt robbed when they were forced out by farmers who could afford fertilisers or even machines. Initially the wilderness was never far away in times of dearth and permitted beekeeping or the hunting of wolves which earned a generous bounty. When stronger iron implements became available, however, the rough ground was ploughed up by entrepreneurs and the peasant opportunities for foraging were reduced. Rich farmers built carts to take wheat to flour mills and bakeries that were given inducements to switch from imported wheat to domestic wheat. Although the breaking of new ground impoverished some peasants to the benefit of large farmers, it still did not make Portugal self-sufficient in grain and only after the world depression of 1930 did government intervene with a food production programme comparable to that tried by Mussolini in Italy.

The nineteenth-century population of southern Portugal was highly stratified even after the abolition of feudal privileges. Owners of great estates made themselves into a distinctive social class, superior to their working neighbours, let alone to their employees. This élite chose its marriage partners with immense care, sought higher education for its children, hired bailiffs to give orders to its workers and avoided any kind of manual work. This provincial aristocracy distanced itself from practising farmers who possessed, managed and worked their own land and acquired literacy and trade skills when necessary. These farmers in their turn did not wear the leather jerkin of the labouring man and chose marriage partners of appropriate status even though they mixed socially with the share-croppers who worked alongside family members. Share-croppers played an important role in clearing the wilderness and sometimes kept up to three-quarters of the crop they grew or even gained ownership of newly broken plots. These share-croppers were considered above the lowest class of peasant society and themselves hired day labourers though they would not deign to take a labourer's daughter as a bride. The hard and insecure life of a farm labourer began at the age of seven when a man-child was sent off as an apprentice to an itinerant shepherd. By the age of fourteen wholly uneducated fieldhands worked on piece rate from first light until dusk except during the harvest season when work went on into the night. When the weather was bad nothing was earned. Few improvements in working conditions occurred until well into the twentieth century.

Social security in rural society was based on charity. Farmers bequeathed clothes to their labourers in their wills, and farm wives bountifully handed out bread and sausage on feast days. The giving of alms to the poor was as ingrained in Catholic society as it had been in Muslim society. The church Misericordia was an important brotherhood which received dues with which to provide welfare for the indigent and hospital beds for the sick. Alms were also given out of fear when groups of able-bodied men, women and children roamed the south in times of unemployment threatening social upheaval. The alternative to begging was stealing, an equally well-established form of social levelling. Stealing from the rich was

30   Water is a scarce resource in much of southern Portugal and was delivered to the villages by donkey, a practice which continued in the twentieth century.

more acceptable among working-class peers than stealing from the poor, a crime associated with outcasts and 'gypsies'. By the late nineteenth century the liberal state found more orthodox methods for curtailing the incipient violence of the underemployed and used some of them on its great public work projects, though at minimal rates of remuneration.

The public works programme adopted in Portugal after 1851 was dramatic. It began with the establishment of a modern post office which issued its first stamps in the name of Maria II shortly before her premature death in 1853. Two years later an electric telegraph was established and within half a century it was carrying almost a million inland telegrams and half a million overseas ones. Greater energy still was required to build the road system that had been so neglected by Pombal when other European countries were adopting macadamised surfaces. When the government of 1851 came to power barely 200 kilometres of all-weather road existed. A month-long traffic census on the main track linking Lisbon to Oporto recorded the laborious passing of 42 carried litters, 50 coaches, 256 donkeys, 3,569 horse riders, 4,313 two-wheel ox carts and 63,406 pedestrians. Thereafter the government used tax revenue to build 200 kilometres of road each year in a network that survived until the advent of the motor lorry in the 1920s. Even more dramatic than the road programme was the initiation of a railway system. This was built with extensive foreign capital, mainly from France, and was designed not only to link Portugal to mainland Europe via Spain but also to speed up internal communications. Spectacular engineering works bridged the great rivers and brought trains by tunnel into the heart of the cities. In Lisbon hydraulic lifts carried passengers from street level up to the platforms on the side of a cliff encased in a pseudo-Manueline palace and at Oporto the station was decorated with exceptionally fine tiled murals.

The political driving force of modernisation was the 'party of re-generation'. It was dominated by an engineer called Fontes Pereira de Melo who towered over Portuguese politics for thirty-five years. He not only planned the public works projects but also travelled in Europe raising the necessary international loans. His party alter-nated in power with the 'historical party' which adopted the same modernising vision but aspired to slightly more democratic ideals from the 1820s whereas the regeneration party inherited the tech-nocratic principles of the 1840s. The widowed king-consort and his sons Pedro V and Luis I recognised the value of alternating the party in power to spread the benefits of office and to lower the tempera-ture of confrontation. Elections usually occurred after a change of government, not before, and were then won by the incoming ad-ministration which manipulated the patronage of the party bosses among the provincial electors. The historical party continued to be influenced by the elderly Marquis of Sá da Bandeira who gradually led it towards the left to become 'reformist' and later 'progressive' before it was overtaken by the rise of socialism and republicanism. It was Sá da Bandeira who presided over a government which in 1869 finally achieved the old liberal ambition of at least nominally outlawing slavery in the Portuguese colonies. In the following year, however, his successor was unable to solve a growing financial crisis resulting from a European economic recession and an unexpected attack of old-style politics brought a *coup d'état* by the now anti-quated Duke of Saldanha.

The year 1870 turned out to be an important turning point in the making of modern Portugal. The comfortable years of early Victorian elegance and peaceful prosperity for the landed aristocracy and the mercantile middle class were undermined, and the élitist two-party democracy of the bourgeois monarchy was temporarily shaken. The turbulence was loosely linked to political change in Europe. The unification of both Germany and Italy led to aspirations for the reunification of Iberia. Amid much controversy the Spanish crown was offered to the Portuguese king-consort in a bid to arrest Spanish republicanism and unite the peninsula. Saldanha was the Portuguese envoy in Madrid at the time and witnessed the potentially subversive threat to his country of either Spanish republicanism or Spanish unification. Even more dramatic signs of impending crisis came from France where the second empire was about to fall, leading to the temporary establishment of a 'communist' administration in the city of Paris. Shortly before that the 'liberal' north had defeated the 'conservative' south in the American civil war. The writing on the wall was enough to persuade a conservative old soldier to return to Lisbon and ride up to the royal palace demanding dictatorial powers to repel the creeping threat of socialism and republicanism. The real threat to Portugal's well-being, however, was more deeply rooted in a world economic recession.

In the 1850s the price of wine had been high and Portugal had enjoyed prosperity and stability. In the 1860s the world demand for Mediterranean produce fell back while the price of imported wheat continued to rise, leaving Portugal uncomfortably squeezed. The recession also affected the textile industry and in 1868 urban protests forced the government to reduce taxation and cut the royal family's civil list. The politicians once again considered economic development strategies which would lessen their external dependence, especially dependence on Britain which had risen to such a dominant position that it bought 80 per cent of Portugal's exports. The reformers recognised that the severe shortage of education would have to be remedied if productivity was to rise. They also acknowledged that they would have to listen to responsible spokesmen for the workers and even admit them into government if they were to defuse the most radical demands for the extension of political rights. Proletarian leaders, however, were divided between those demanding improved conditions for the industrial élite, and those seeking

31   Modern Portugal produced half the world's supply of
cork, stripped from the trunks of cork oaks and formerly
exported in sheets or hand-worked for bottle corks and household appliances.

a broad political platform for the working class. The bourgeoisie
was thus able to regroup as the economy picked up and the radical
challenge was deferred for a generation.

The return of the old parliamentarians after 1871 was marked by
a growth in manufacturing as machine production rivalled craft production. Imports of machinery rose tenfold in six years until investment in machinery amounted to one-third of all registered company
capital. With Fontes Pereira de Melo back in office share speculation reached fever pitch though his rivals feared the unbridled influx
of influential foreign capital. Foreign investors supported railways

which were guaranteed by government, but Portuguese investors had to put their capital into genuine risk ventures and keep an eye on the price of wine to assess the likely demand for their products. For a time wine prices were high as French vineyards were decimated by disease and Portuguese wines captured new markets. Agricultural incomes also rose with increased access to cheap and reliable railway transport. At the same time industrial production trebled under the impact of 'regeneration capitalism'. In 1851 there had been only 1,000 horse-power units of motor capacity in all Portugal. Thirty years later there were 9,000 horse-power units of installed capacity, the cotton industry had expanded to employ 1,000 looms, and small factories making glass, ceramic tiles and cork furnishings were thriving. Portugal still had only a very modest industrial sector but it was growing and becoming politically significant.

During the era of prosperity that preceded renewed crises in 1890 Portuguese management and labour each learnt new strategies in their confrontations with each other. When strikes broke out in the Oporto tobacco industry management responded by dismissing skilled workers and installing simplified machines that could be operated by child labour. In industries where one-quarter of the labour force was below the age of fifteen children constituted a constant threat to adult workers seeking improved pay and conditions. The bargaining power of labour was similarly undermined in the cork industry where British firms used children even for such dangerous tasks as the cutting of bottle corks which had to be pared with razor knives at the rate of hundreds of corks per hour. Female labour was also used to undermine male wages, and in Lisbon the tobacco workers' union refused to admit women since they were often willing to work short shifts when the union was trying to establish a guaranteed working day of at least ten hours to ensure a living wage. Strikes and street demonstrations became a central part of the generalised crisis of 1890. This crisis was also associated with a decline in wine exports, with the abolition of Brazilian slavery, with the loss of the Congo and Zambezi trading basins in Africa, and with a revolution which overthrew the South American branch of the house of Braganza.

The great crisis of 1890 brought a debate among politicians, since continued by historians, as to what the best Portuguese strategy

32   In 1886 an obelisk commemorating the Portuguese
restoration of independence in 1640 was erected in the Lisbon
public gardens and the broad 'Avenue of Liberty' was built,
which eventually led to the park named after King Edward
VII and to the city's elegant suburbs. (Photograph taken in the
1950s.)

should have been to escape from the shackles of underdevelopment and economic dependency. The received wisdom was that Portugal suffered from the domination of Great Britain. The argument was most succinctly expressed by Eça de Queirós, the leading novelist of Portugal's brilliant generation of Victorian intellectuals. Everything, he said, is imported: 'laws, ideas, philosophies, topics of debate, aesthetic values, science, style, industry, fashion, manners, jokes, everything reaches us in small crates on the mail steamer'. His case was overstated for although nineteenth-century Portugal lacked investment and infrastructure by comparison with Britain, or even with pre-industrial France and Germany, it was not substantially different from the rest of Europe and the politicians of regeneration had been implementing a serious programme of modernisation. By 1890, however, Portugal had begun to fall behind, and by 1913 it was significantly retarded by European economic standards though not by world standards.

The received explanation for Portugal's backwardness begins with its alleged failure to build adequate tariff barriers to protect its infant industries, succumbing instead to British pressure to continue to supply raw materials and buy manufactures. A second structural defect of the Portuguese economy was thought to be in the pattern of landownership where neither the great estates of the south nor the fragmented holdings of the north were conducive to agricultural modernisation. More seriously still the slow rate of modernisation was blamed on an educational stagnation which the sweeping away of the *ancien régime* had not adequately remedied. In matters of finance the upper bourgeoisie remained anachronistically tied to the aristocracy and preferred to invest its money in land, buildings and the pursuit of noble titles. As in third world countries much of the lower middle class sought security through the salaries of public service rather than in small-scale productive enterprises. Another restraint was the old problem that government income remained linked to customs revenue imposed on imports and exports. As a result treasury inertia condoned the influence of the trading bourgeoisie and did not press for a self-reliant economic nationalism that would require new revenue systems. Portugal's economic problems were further compounded by the fact that in the dominant agricultural industry poor soils and an indifferent climate made it difficult

33   Emigration dominated the lives of working-class
Portuguese between the mid-nineteenth century and the world
recession of the early 1930s. These women and children are
on their way to Brazil.

for farmers to earn enough to benefit from the 'nitrogen revolution' which was transforming productivity in northern Europe even
where plots were small and landlords absent.

Revised ideas about Portugal's underdevelopment point out that
the government did adopt a protectionist policy with tariffs as high
as any in Europe or the United States. It is also pointed out that
Portugal had a lower level of international trade than many comparable states with barely 7 per cent of the national product linked to
foreign business compared to twice that proportion elsewhere. The
idea that import-substitution would be the ideal form of industry in a
small country was tenaciously retained, though the Portuguese market was too small for economies of scale to apply in many fields of
production. The entire Portuguese market for machines and spares,
for instance, offered less business than that carried out by a single
British engineering firm in Ipswich, and Portuguese steel consumption of 40,000 tons was less than the output of one British mill.
More strikingly still the average Portuguese only bought half the

European consumption of cotton textiles, paying for them only 1 per cent of the national income, and so textiles were not the obvious basis for a growth industry nor were they a foreign exchange drain of crippling proportions. Wealth was potentially more forthcoming from specialist local industries such as cork, which neglected many opportunities and continued to export over 90 per cent of its production in unfinished form, or sardines which could be canned and so compete with the very profitable high protein dairy and meat industries of northern Europe. The dominant economic sector, however, and the one which caused governments to rise and fall, remained the wine industry.

In theory wine production could have stimulated a whole range of local industries. Modernised vineyards generated a local market for ploughs, sprayers, barrels and pruning scissors as well as improving the viability of the railways. Vines yielded three times the revenue of wheat and could be grown both as a supplement to subsistence and as an estate crop. Doubling the national output would theoretically have enhanced government export revenue and satisfied the profit demands of the dominant merchant class. But the international wine trade became stubbornly static at the end of the nineteenth century, rising only 3 per cent per annum when agrarian commodities in other countries expanded two or three times as fast. The quality of Portuguese table wines remained variable, and subject to none of the quality controls that had been imposed on fortified wines. The alcohol content of Lisbon wines was higher than was preferred in markets accustomed to French and Italian wines. Worst of all nineteenth-century Portuguese farmers were not given the educational skills to develop a co-operative movement which could introduce new techniques to enhance production. They were also unable to train competent co-operative managers to improve marketing and thereby transforming the backwardness of the rural economy. The stagnation in the wine industry began at the same time that more immediate crises beset Portugal in 1890.

The major consequence of the failure of agricultural development was the flight of people from the land. Economic refugees with some education gained white collar jobs in Lisbon and Oporto and both cities doubled in size under the bourgeois monarchy. Ten times as many people, however, were forced to leave the country altogether, legally or clandestinely, and take ship for Brazil. A 'white slave trade' was organised and its agents bribed and corrupted emigration officers, sea captains and consular visa clerks. One tiny sailing vessel of 200 tons was caught smuggling out 428 close-packed transatlantic emigrants whose living conditions were no better than those of black slaves on the middle passage from Africa. In 1888 the abolition of Brazilian slavery intensified the efforts of labour recruiters in Portugal until 25,000 people a year were emigrating officially, and many more clandestinely, to the dismay of farmers who were seasonally short of hands for the harvest. The government was ambivalent about stopping the haemorrhage since migrant savings were sent back to families in Portugal on a scale which kept the country solvent. The only attractive alternative to permitting emigration to continue was to create a new empire, this time in Africa.

The significance of the colonies to nineteenth-century Portugal has been a subject of much debate with some historians seeing them as the uneconomic fruit of national wistfulness and others as the basis of a new dynamic thrust to replace the partial loss of economic access to Brazil. In Africa an old Portuguese presence survived thanks mainly to creole communities of largely African descent but Portuguese culture. The most distinctive and influential creole communities lived on the archipelagos of Cape Verde and São Tomé where pidgin Portuguese developed a written as well as an oral literature. In Mozambique the creoles had long-standing ties with India and attracted a significant Asian community with great commercial influence. In Angola the black creole community spoke Portuguese, adopted Catholicism, accepted civil law, staffed the rudimentary colonial administration, led the colonial armies and recognised the sovereignty of the Braganza dynasty. Creole traders also sold slaves, at first officially but later under the guise of 'contract workers', to the tiny but profitable offshore coffee and cocoa plantations of São Tomé. When the liberals abolished the royal trading monopolies in Africa creoles and immigrant convicts took up ivory trading and also found a ready market for beeswax candles, orchilla dyes and root rubber, none of which was sufficiently lucrative, however, to encourage the founding of an empire. Itinerant Portuguese merchants preferred to develop river transport, money lending and rubber trading in the Amazon rather than risk going to Africa.

34 The 'scramble for Africa' left Portugal in control of five colonies. The largest, Angola, was opened up to mining and planting with British railways, Belgian commerce, national steamships and a new deep-water harbour at Lobito Bay, imagined here in a contemporary advertisement.

The economic crisis of 1870 had been the watershed which changed upper-class Portuguese attitudes to Africa. Although the crisis appeared momentary, the balance between the Mediterranean world of wines and fruits and the northern world of industry and dairy produce had decisively shifted against Portugal and the search for new overseas wealth took on a fresh urgency. The barons of liberalism met in the Victorian splendour of their new Geographical Society club house to listen to the exploits of African explorers, to remember the glories of past conquistadores, and to plan new enterprises in the tropics. By 1880 well-publicised visible imports of rubber and ivory from the colonies exceeded the cotton, sugar and hides from Brazil, though the invisible remittances from migrants to South America made Brazil economically more important than the empire right up until the great depression of 1930. Nevertheless even the development of quinine, which made Africa a rather less pestilential place in which to live than hitherto, could not persuade either illiterate emigrants or shrewd businessmen to share the enthusiasm for Africa that armchair geographers enjoyed. Some politicians, however, persisted with the dream, seeing the creation of an empire as one viable alternative to being swallowed again by Spain. Spain could have provided Portugal with raw materials such as iron and coal, and with a viable local export market on the new railways, but Spain might also have encouraged social instability and the old barons therefore preferred to explore the untested alternatives of Africa.

Portugal's dream of a transcontinental empire in Africa was destroyed in two short moves by two rival nations with similar ambitions to its own, Belgium and the Cape Colony in South Africa. The king of the Belgians, Leopold II, was a Saxe-Coburg cousin of the royal family who successfully laid claim to the whole Congo–Zaire hinterland of Portugal's west coast trading factories. In a carefully prepared diplomatic swoop he assured himself of a million square miles of ivory hunting and rubber collecting and gained the ancient and very rich copper mines of Katanga. A fragment of Portuguese national self-esteem was preserved by the granting of territorial rights over the Bay of Cabinda, north of the Zaire estuary, but only sixty years later did this become the richest of all Portugal's colonies when oil was found in an offshore strike. The second diplomatic coup which deprived Portugal of mineral wealth and markets in Africa came from the semi-autonomous British colony of the Cape where the tough diamond magnate, Cecil Rhodes, secured British help in laying claim to the Zambezi basin. He astutely used the admirers of Livingstone's evangelising enterprises to stir up colonial jingoism in Britain and so force the prime minister, Salisbury, to order Portugal

AS MENINAS

35 This turn-of-the-century cartoon shows an elderly man carrying the imperial poems of Camões, accompanied by colonial 'daughters' from China, Indonesia, Mozambique and Angola, and eyed enviously by British and German suitors anxious to partition Portugal's overseas possessions.

to withdraw from the hinterland of Mozambique. To Rhodes' dismay Portugal was able to retain the coastal ports that were later to provide access to his mines and plantations, but the rose-coloured map, and the Portuguese company plans for a Royal Transafrica Railway, had to be shelved.

Although modest in scope the African empire of the 1890s still had to be explored and conquered. In Mozambique the wars were brutal but short and Portugal then handed effective administration of most of the territory to foreign companies which were given varying unsupervised rights to collect poll taxes, conscript migrant male workers, and force women to grow compulsory rice and cotton crops for private enterprises. One of the companies retained its administrative responsibility until 1940, leaving a lingering aura of harsh exploitation, while another was given a regional monopoly in conscripting mine workers for South Africa that continued throughout the colonial era. In Angola Portugal also adopted policies similar to slavery in order to build roads and grow coffee. The sale of indentured workers involved such inhumanity, however, that it brought an international outcry in the last years of the monarchy. Humanitarian criticism in 1910 and imperial losses in 1890 meant that the empire had a controversial profile and played a significant role in the rise of Portuguese republicanism.

Two 'imperial' factors speeded the Portuguese towards republicanism. In 1889 Brazil provided a revolutionary model by overthrowing the American branch of the Braganzas and establishing a republic. In the following year anti-British riots broke out in Oporto which shook the throne of the European Braganzas as well. Although nominally about the loss of Central Africa, the 1890 riots were a well-orchestrated litany of despair at the squeeze of the economic recession and the impotence of a small dependent country. The old rulers of regeneration needed to reform the political franchise fast if they were to keep ahead of revolutionary demands, and more especially of demands for the removal of the allegedly pro-British royal family. The pressure of republicanism continued to grow in the 1890s with the expansion of the industrial proletariat. Republicans were intermittent allies of the early socialists in seeking support among the still unenfranchised urban majority. More dangerously still republicanism began to take root among the army, traditionally loyal to its royal commander-in-chief. It was junior military officers who triggered off the *coup d'état* of 1910 which ushered in the republic. Working-class influences were soon eclipsed, however, as middle-class intellectuals and lawyers took charge much as they had done in the revolution of 1820.

Republicanism had been a permanent strand of Portuguese political thought throughout the nineteenth century, but the royal charter was sufficiently flexible to satisfy the conservatives while keeping jacobinism at bay. Republican ideals had been voiced by the radicals of September 1836 and in the Oporto uprising of 1846 but after 1851 the compromises and class alliances which ended the revolution led to nearly half a century of Victorian stability before a professional class of doctors, teachers and public servants began to mobilise a republican movement. By the time they did so they faced political rivalry from a different republican strand of machine minders, cashiers and market gardeners. Still lower in the social hierarchy popular antagonism to the monarchy was allied to the search for trade union power and the right to strike. Although the parliamentary barons might bracket republicanism and socialism together as

36 Carlos I ascended the throne in 1889 and was acclaimed at the city hall in Lisbon, as shown in this contemporary engraving. He was assassinated eighteen years later in an adjacent street.

37   The republicans stole a march on the monarchists in 1880
by adopting the poet Camões as their patriotic hero on the
tercentenary of his death.

dangerous subversion, in practice the rival ideologies had difficulty
in achieving a radical consensus and bridging the gap between socialist workers and petty bourgeois republicans. The republicans
gained their first political success not in the field of social reform
but in the field of intellectual nationalism. They captured the initiative in 1880 by organising a celebration of the tercentenary
of Camões, Portugal's most patriotic poet. With the support of

professors and generals they gained in respectability, went on to win their first seat in parliament and to found a national newspaper, *O Trabalho*, edited by Elias Garcia, a distinguished freemason.

Republicans were given another opportunity to express their patriotic leadership during the riots over the British ultimatum of 1890. Violent protest escalated beyond the control of the moderate leadership, however, and culminated in a republican rebellion in Oporto in 1891. The monarchical politicians were given an opportunity to fight back, crushed the uprising, and instituted a tight press censorship which 'corked' future expressions of public feeling. Opponents of government were accused of anarchism and exiled to the colonies while the king was defended by the bayonets of reorganised regiments of guards. The parliamentary constituencies were then 'gerrymandered' to reduce the power of the cities and by 1901 the old republican party of the intellectuals was excluded from parliament and soon wound itself up. A mere eight years later, however, the Portuguese monarchy unexpectedly fell and politicians rushed to assume the republican mantle. They had neglected to recognise that despite the ennoblement of members of the middle class as a new landowning aristocracy with seats in the provinces, the power of Portugal remained firmly in the cities, and more especially in the capital where urban political influence was growing and changing.

The republican revolution of 1910 was a Lisbon revolution. Half the country's teachers, doctors and accountants lived there, and many of its tailors, chemists and coal merchants. Thirty per cent of industrial employees worked in or near the city where they could earn ten times the wage of a farm labourer. The city had 688 barber's shops, almost as many bawdy houses, and innumerable taverns where an all-male political culture thrived on dozens of newspapers read by men who had twice the literacy rate of Oporto and four times that of the provinces. Members of the rumour-mongering petty bourgeoisie felt their status and experience to be humiliated by daily indignities arising from the servility owed to priests, politicians and employers. The Latin street culture of Lisbon became increasingly volatile and even more liable than that of Oporto to burst into demonstrations. Across the river in the industrial zone workers increased in militancy as well as in numbers, though illiterate people in villages beyond had little awareness of the monarchy and no inkling that it was about to collapse under the impulse of a military conspiracy.

The junior army officers who initiated the overthrow of the monarchy and the declaration of the republic belonged to a secret society introduced into Portugal from Italy in the early nineteenth century. Instead of borrowing their symbolism from cathedral builders, like the upper-class freemasons, they used the language of forestry and charcoal-burning, calling themselves the 'carbonari'. The blindfolded initiates swore to overthrow tyrants and to obey only the commands of the order as relayed through its hierarchy of cells. They shared a common hostility to the church and reinforced the anti-clerical backbone of republicanism. The leaders were of humble class origins though a few may have belonged to the upper class and it has even been suggested that the quixotic Duke of Saldanha, a former grandmaster of a dissident masonic lodge, may have been initiated into a carbonari cell at one time in his eventful career. Of the 400 carbonari imprisoned in the last years of the monarchy a majority were factory workers and only a sprinkling were journalists, civil servants and soldiers. The scale of their subversion in the army was limited to anarchist sympathisers anxious to throw off the tyranny of their superior officers as much as the tyranny of the king. The navy, by contrast, was a significant source of republicanism and the carbonari cells were active when the ship *Admastor* gave the signal for the revolution to roll on 4 October 1910.

Portugal was only the third country in Europe, after France and Switzerland, to proclaim a lasting republican government. The model was a French one, but the republicans had to ascertain that Britain's Liberal government would neither intervene to restore the Braganzas, nor permit Spain to do so. When the revolution came they were reassured that the British foreign office considered it to be quite orderly, giving no cause for interference. The republican leaders, on the other hand, were caught completely unawares by the speed of events. The king had dined in state with the visiting president of Brazil before going home to play bridge. His game was interrupted when he was advised to leave the palace in haste and take ship for England from a lonely beach. Meanwhile in the city two regiments that had been infiltrated by carbonari arrested their officers in their pyjamas and issued weapons to a half-hearted mob outside the barracks. Republican politicians, waking to find that they had unexpectedly inherited a revolution, ordered the patrolling of streets, the protecting of property and the repression of any signs of anarchism. Lisbon changed hands uneventfully and the rest of the country accepted telegraphic instructions to haul down the royal flag and hoist the republican one. The provinces were unenthusiastic but did not resist. The army did not try to save its king and let him go without a struggle feeling that however many regimental dinners he had graced they had not enhanced his charisma or his popularity. A trade union newspaper barely mentioned the event.

Although the republic had been the child of the lower middle class, it was immediately taken over by the upper middle class which adopted the battle cry of anti-clericalism as a unifying urban slogan. The intellectuals appointed one of the most prestigious of their number, Teófilo Braga, as president, but the greatest of the republican leaders was Afonso Costa who became minister of justice of the Provisional Government. He was a lawyer who had taught at Coimbra and had founded a faculty of laws in Lisbon. In 1891 his youthful republicanism had led him to take part in the abortive uprising in Oporto, in 1905 he was sworn into the freemasons and by 1908 he was a member of parliament. Once in office his vision of freedom led to the curtailment of religious privilege, the banning of clerical dress outside of churches, the second dissolution of the monasteries, the separation of church and state, the acceptance of divorce and a modest recognition of the rights of women and children. His next step was to take over the ministry of finance, reform the currency, reduce the public debt, and create a prestigious 'grande école' for commerce. He was unable, however, even when he became prime minister, to match the huge expectations which the republic had unleashed among the proletariat with the crisis-ridden resources of the economy. In foreign policy he favoured close ties with Britain which put his popularity at risk. He accepted that only Britain could protect Portugal's colonies in Africa from German cupidity, even though the price to be paid was the raising of an expeditionary force to be sent to France in 1917. This financially and politically ruinous decision to enter the war brought about the downfall of his government, though he personally remained a commanding presence who was sent to the Versailles peace conference and then to Geneva where

38   In the revolution of 1910 armed republicans barricaded
the streets but nevertheless took care to defend private property.

he eventually became president of the League of Nations. With the rise of fascist influence in Portugal he remained in exile, reviled by some as the persecutor of the church and idolised by others as the enlightened leader who broke with Portugal's archaic institutions.

The clearest contrast to the democratic republicanism of Afonso Costa was the military authoritarianism of Sidónio Pais. His personal role in the history of the republic was short since he was cut down by assassination within a year of establishing his Prussian-style regime. In the long term, however, it was his brand of dictatorship rather than the humane alternatives adopted during the republican years between 1910 and 1926 which made their mark on twentieth-century Portugal. Sidónio Pais did not emerge as a fully-fledged dictator without antecedents. The last years of the monarchy had thrown up a previous dictator on whom later authoritarian rulers could model themselves. In 1907 King Carlos had bypassed parliament to appoint his own prime minister. Ironically the king's programme had been a liberal one, influenced by the change of climate in Anglo-Saxon politics where the avoidance of revolution was achieved by controlled social reform. The parliamentarians were incensed and their protests led to royal repression. Instead of creating a reformed democracy, with new social justice, the king's minister created Portugal's first modern dictatorship. The result was to enhance republican violence and the first victim was the king himself, assassinated in 1908 along with his eldest son.

Ten years later the Sidónio Pais dictatorship had no liberal intent when it overthrew Afonso Costa in 1917. Sidónio Pais was a former freemason who persecuted freemasons, a former republican minister who despised the republic, a former lecturer in mathematics who had been seduced by military life, and Portugal's former ambassador to wartime Germany. His long residence in Prussia marked his political style when he unilaterally appointed himself executive president of the republic after his return from Berlin. His *coup d'état* met with approval from those who had resented British demands that Portugal should confiscate the German fleet at Lisbon and send 55,000 men to fight and die in the trenches of France. He won support from monarchists, who hoped he would call the young King Manuel II back from exile, from bishops who hoped he would restore the privileges of the church, from landowners who hoped he would restore inequalities of wealth, from industrialists who hoped he would repress the trade unions in spite of the fact that it was their popular clamour against the war which had helped him gain acceptance. Sidónio Pais could not, however, square the political circle of contradictory demands and when he faced serious bread riots he repressed them with bloodshed and moved to impose ever more dictatorial decisions. His experiment in presidentialism ended within a year when he was assassinated on his way to Oporto to face a monarchist rebellion.

The short-lived dictatorship of Sidónio Pais was not typical of the republic. The hallmark was democracy rather than discipline, carrying on in a third phase the reforming achievements of the revolution of 1820–51 and of the bourgeois monarchy of 1851–1910. After a century of modest liberalism, however, oppressive inequality remained widespread, and the republic, for all its middle-class caution, tried to continue the slow erosion of privilege. It was its success rather than its failure which caused the conservatives to regroup their ranks. The republicans earned the unpopularity of confronting the post-war financial crisis with austere realism and by the middle 1920s had put the economy back on a reasonably stable footing. The budget savings, however, were inimical to the interests of pretentiously inflated senior cadres of the army who orchestrated a campaign of denigration against civilian politicians which eventually paved the way for a military *coup d'état* launched from the ultra-Catholic city of Braga in 1926. The real failure of the republic, however, was not its neglect of the army, or even its persecution of the church, but its inability to recognise that Lisbon was not Portugal and that the well-being of the people depended on agrarian renewal and not on the petty squabbles of class fractions in the cities. Agrarian immobility, stagnant production, wasteful latifundia and fragmented peasant plots all led to the continuation, and even increase, of high levels of emigration by unhappy, illiterate farm workers whose conditions of life were only little better than those of the Chinese 'coolies' who were beginning to come on to the international labour market.

Under the republic the population of Portugal continued to grow despite unprecedented levels of emigration, despite the loss of 60,000 lives in the great influenza pandemic of 1918, and despite the killing and wounding of 10,000 able-bodied men during the First World War. The rising population meant that the question of wheat continued to dominate the political agenda. The protectionist legislation of the last years of the monarchy, including a 'famine law' of 1899, had not raised the price of domestic wheat enough to stimulate the country to self-sufficiency despite extensive new ploughing and some introduction of steam threshing. While politicians debated the virtue of buying cheap foreign wheat for their urban proletariat the war came to disrupt shipping and bring bitter bread riots. After the war the politicians bought social calm by subsidising the flour mills but still failed to increase wheat production and so eliminate the food deficit. Many southern landlords continued to be Lisbon absentees with little interest in modernising their farms. A proposal was made in 1925 by socialists, supported by communists and anarchists, that control of the land should be handed to those who worked it. Such radicalism was before its time and was swept away for fifty years in the *coup d'état* of 1926.

While the republic neglected agriculture and allowed the labour force of Portugal to drain abroad rather than revitalise the provinces it did bring significant change to its urban supporters. An improved status was given to women despite the prevailing Latin culture of machismo, and wage-earning men were able, with socialist campaigning, to jump ahead of the rest of Europe for a few years by obtaining an eight-hour working day. Freedom of thought replaced the moral restrictions of the priests and the political limits of the censors and illiteracy was reduced by a limited widening of access to education. Much thought was devoted to the last of the monarchy's legacies, the African empire. In Africa the republic created thousands of jobs as petty functionaries for lower middle-class supporters in the towns whom it could not reward with salaried posts at home. Carpet-baggers poured into the colonies seeking sinecures rather than carrying skills and capital. They came into headlong confrontation with the old creole bureaucrats whose jobs they demanded with racist self-justification. In colonial matters the republic was far from liberal and its greatest proconsul, Norton de Matos, continued to justify neo-slavery in Angola as a means of building an economic infrastructure and supplying cheap black labour to prospective colonial investors.

39   Barber shops in republican Lisbon created a typical décor which was long retained.

The republican government in Portugal, like the first Labour government in Britain a few years later, was astonishingly conservative in its fiscal policy. The street leaders of the revolution were photographed with unintended irony as a dispossessed mob defending the commercial banks of the propertied class from looters. The defence of conventional values went even deeper in a republican search for respectability and a pre-Keynesian balanced budget. Initially the new politicians had scruples about devaluing the currency and enlarging the national debt, though the war radically forced their hand. The republican money managers had one particularly severe stroke of bad luck when they were caught up in one of the biggest financial swindles of the age. The ultra-respectable British printing firm of Waterlow and Sons was fraudulently persuaded to print large quantities of Portuguese banknotes which the government had not authorised, thereby irreversibly undermining confidence in the currency and causing savings and investments to take refuge abroad. By the time the republic fell the national reserves were uncomfortably low. Those who feared most for their financial well-being were not the speculators who had profited from the war, but those on fixed incomes who saw their modest means whittled away by austerity and inflation. They became a fertile recruiting ground for right-wing activists who studied the rise of fascism. Petty functionaries whose jobs had been created by the republic but whose salaries did not subsequently keep pace with prices were ready to welcome policies which repressed the Lisbon proletariat which had doubled in size under the republic and was nurturing the communist party.

Religion was a dominant preoccupation of the republic. The church, which had been so severely persecuted in the 1830s, had been revitalised in the 1870s after the first Vatican Council. Portuguese religious intolerance revived with new saints, new religious orders and new persecution of free thinkers. Monasteries were once again legalised and even the Jesuits regained their control over the education of the conservative élite and the pious royal household. The republican backlash against clericalism led not only to the second dissolution of the religious orders but even to the retirement of many parish priests whose livings had survived the previous attack on the church. Church and state were legally separated in 1911, following the 1905 lead given by France, and civil weddings were introduced. Protesting bishops were again exiled, relations with the Vatican were again severed, but the faithful, especially in the rural north, continued defiantly to attend mass. The intensity of antagonism to the church derived in part from the traditional anti-clericalism of Portuguese freemasons. Under the republic the hundred-odd masonic lodges enrolled 4,000 members of the élite, including a majority of those who served as prime minister. Antagonism to the church was tempered by Portugal's entry into the First World War which led politicians to recognise the value of organised religion and even caused them to allow a return of the Jesuits. Catholics, however, never fully trusted the republic and many of them were ready to work for its demise. The Catholic soldiers who eventually toppled the republic in 1926 also outlawed the masonic lodges, though not without protest from some of their fellow officers.

The republican attack on the church, like the liberal one in the previous century, left a need for state education. The monarchy had reformed secondary education for the few, but it was the republic which extended primary education, opened mass-literacy classes, encouraged extramural 'university' courses, and sponsored seminars and debates. It also encouraged publishers to produce literature in paperback editions for working men and allowed an abridged edition of *Das Kapital* to circulate, thereby provoking right-wing sections of society, especially Coimbra graduates, into believing that education was detrimental to national well-being. One influential school of political thought that emerged from the broadening of education was the 'New Harvest' (*Seara Nova*) founded in 1921. The movement supported democratic socialism and international pacifism and was the ideological rival of 'Portuguese Fundamentalism' (*Integralismo Lusitano*) which opposed individual rights, popular sovereignty and liberal concepts of economic progress. The fundamentalists even rejected the constitutionalism of the exiled Manuel II and proposed a Miguelite absolutist as candidate for the vacant throne. The fundamentalists also fed some of the European anti-semitism of the 1920s into Portuguese politics.

The republic came to an end in 1926. Throughout its short life strands of opposition had evolved which aimed to capture the state and lead it in a different direction. The church was one of the more powerful of those strands, but it was relatively slow to regain its influence and was feared by new-style nationalists who wanted all loyalty to be directed towards themselves. The lower middle class was another of the sectors that opposed the grand ideas of the intelligentsia and welcomed a government which they hoped would preserve their small savings and guarantee their white collar jobs in preference to those of the labouring masses. The army officers who had been undermined by the junior officers in the revolution of 1910 were anxious to restore their influence and enhance their status if not their active military responsibilities. It was they who had the guns to make the first move against a republic that they had persistently undermined and denigrated until their challenge was likely to attract enough acclaim to be successful.

6

The dictatorship and the African empire

The great depression of 1930 affected Portugal as profoundly as any country in Europe. The external dimension of the economy had hitherto continued to reach two ways, northward to Britain which supplied consumer goods and southward to Brazil which supplied money in the form of savings sent home by emigrants. The depression ended this system of two-way dependency and forced Portugal to become more self-reliant at home and to seek new trading partners abroad. The domestic change involved a severe retrenchment in the scope of government. The liberal reforms of the bourgeois monarchy and of the republic were abandoned and a new autocratic oligarchy gained ascendancy which curtailed workers' rights, restricted expenditure on education and services and repressed political opinions with an increase of police surveillance. Politics were increasingly dominated by a single dictator who satisfied the aspirations of the old-style army officers while distancing them from the practice of politics, Upper middle-class Catholic civilians formed a new generation of politicians who quietly admired the disciplinarian politics of fascist Italy and Nazi Germany. They also looked southward with a view to extracting new wealth from the African empire both as a closed market for wines and textiles and as a cheap source of tropical sugar and cotton. The austerity of the inter-war dictatorship was increased by the outbreak of the Second World War and the further curtailment of seaborne commerce even among neutral nations. In 1943, as in 1917, Portugal was forced to compromise its neutrality and support the British war effort against Germany, this time by opening military bases on the Azores Islands to the Atlantic allies. After the war continuation of the dictatorship was tolerated by the allies because of its anticommunist stance, though as a non-democratic country Portugal was initially excluded from the United Nations. Stern government prevented a civil war such as afflicted post-war Greece but did not attract investment and industry such as revitalised post-war Italy. By the 1960s rapid social change was brought about by a renewed vitality in the African empire and by the European 'economic miracle' which created a large market for Portuguese migrant workers. The ruling oligarchy proved sufficiently flexible to ride the change until 1974 by which time both industrialists and the military wanted to force the pace of modernisation. After a bloodless *coup d'état* a short-lived military regime abandoned the by now embattled empire and turned Portugal to face the European Common Market. Democratic politicians resumed the responsibilities they had lost in 1926.

The inter-war history of Portugal during the great depression is so intimately bound up with the political ideology of its prime minister that historians cannot altogether avoid adopting a biographical approach. António Salazar was the son of a farm manager whose burningly ambitious mother sent him to a seminary in search of the best available education. His road to the priesthood was not a smooth one and although he was known back in the village as 'Father António' he never progressed beyond the minor vows. His law studies were more successful, and, in 1917, he began his teaching career at Coimbra university. He was a fastidious young man who had, according to some, a liking for women and champagne but a constant anxiety that good dining with his urban friends was an excessive strain on the budget of his rural family. He husbanded his minor investments with great care, bought small plots of land in his village, and shared modest quarters with a priest who was later to become the cardinal-patriarch of Lisbon, Dom Manuel Cerejeira. He joined the conservative Catholic party and wrote articles on national bookkeeping for the press. In 1921 he stood successfully for parliament but kept his seat only for a day and took an aloof attitude to the politicians in Lisbon, preferring to associate with the arrogant élite of Coimbra. From his ivory tower he built up a mystique about his financial omniscience. He derided the republicans for

40 Salazar used the press of the 1920s to foster his aura of
financial infallibility, and in alliance with the army and the
church he 'reigned' as prime minister from 1932 to 1968.

their incompetence and undermined the economic self-confidence of
the generals who replaced them in 1926. When they sought his advice he kept his distance, turning down a ministerial post after a few
days' trial, and becoming ever more Olympian in his pronounce-
ments. He finally persuaded the military that he and he alone could
manage the country's accounts. His terms for accepting the ministry of finance in 1928 were a complete treasury control over all
other ministries. Once in power he survived there for forty years,
occasionally calling the bluff of the generals by threatening to resign
and leave them to their own devices again, and surviving more than
a dozen plots or attempted coups by more junior members of the
armed forces.

The regime created by Salazar, and which he christened 'the new
state', was contemporary with the regimes of Mussolini in Italy and
Primo de Rivera the Elder in Spain and was commonly described by
its opponents as a fascist system of government. Such loose usage of

the term 'fascist' fails to illuminate the specific nature of Portuguese government in the 1930s and its contrasts of substance and style with both the other dictatorships of the western Mediterranean. The common aversion to pluralist liberal democracy, and the violent treatment of opponents, masked differences of ideology and above all the absence of any Portuguese mass party which demagogues could rouse to attack 'public enemies'. Even in his early years Salazar was reluctant to call the Lisbon crowds on to the streets and when he did so his speeches were wooden by comparison with those of his charismatic contemporaries in other countries. Instead of being visible he became reclusive and his propaganda machine presented him as a wise and monkish father, the saviour of the nation, pictured on posters with a crusader's sword in his hand or written into history books as the patriotic successor to the liberating hero of the nation, John IV of Braganza. The violent repression of alternative visions was undertaken discreetly by trained police agents and not by Nazi-style mobs. Yet similarities with fascism were evident and despite all his acclaim of Christian morality after the atheism of the republic, Salazar founded concentration camps for dissidents and decreed forced labour for the unemployed. A critical French observer, Jacques Georgel, dubbed him 'a *petit-bourgeois* monocrat' rather than a true fascist.

The Portuguese regime should not be given a fascist label because it was totalitarian, police-run, corporative, anti-liberal, anti-democratic, anti-parliamentary, anti-collectivist, and disdainful of opponents whom it was willing to eliminate physically . . . It was a fascism deprived of all the attributes of fascism; a kind of travesty governed pettily by a man of extraordinary power-lust who lived in solitude for forty years and felt ill if he had to meet a group. The man claimed to be chosen by destiny for an exceptional mission, a man of burning pride behind a façade of modesty, a man who wished to prove his genius through an entirely idiosyncratic concept of the happiness of his people, a man who, all told, brought his country and its people to ruin.

Jacques Georgel, *Le Salazarisme: Histoire et Bilan 1926–1974* (Paris, 1981) p. 302, translated.

The question that needs to be faced is how did an apparently lone Catholic lecturer in accountancy, opposed to all economic theories of modernisation and development, gain such power in the depression and retain it throughout the Second World War and for many years beyond. The answer is to be found by analysing his very skilled juggling of the interests of the army, the urban middle class, the monarchists and the church. The great ideals that were hammered home by the government's propaganda were patriotism, paternalism and prudence. Patriotism was epitomised by a rejection of the republic and all its values and by a new enthusiasm for Portugal's role as one of the 'great powers' in the African colonies. Paternalism involved an absolute and unquestioning respect for authority and all its agents, including the restored Catholic church. Prudence was enshrined in the virtues of thrift and fortitude for workers and peasants but did not apply to the leisured class who dined well and slept late. Such an agenda satisfied a majority of the army officers who had brought Salazar to power, though not their masonic brethren whose alternative anti-Catholic caste was repressed. The programme also gave Salazar the power to tackle radically if painfully the great slump in Mediterranean exports which decimated the economy. An iron social control kept order when rural employment fell. Hunger threatened, tuberculosis spread, childbearing and infant mortality rose, emigration was closed, but the government was determined not to use the public purse to provide welfare or medical facilities.

The despairing acceptance of a poverty that was closer to the standards of tropical Africa than to those of temperate Europe was assisted by the senior levels of the traditional church hierarchy. The relationship between the dictatorship and the church was complex since the church expected to regain all its old authority under a strongly Catholic politician but the politician was determined to ensure the primacy of the state. They agreed on the need for obedient quiescence by the poor and collaborated in fostering the mystical cult of Fátima which had arisen out of the republican persecutions. As the myth evolved it presented a shrouded vision of apocalypse with children as the chosen envoys of the Virgin Mary and the pope as the guardian of the undisclosed message. Fear was broadcast in ripples among the superstitious and pilgrims began to trek to Fátima on foot or even on their knees. The church encouraged the hysterical dimensions of religious practice to the detriment of more thoughtful forms of worship and the regime adopted Fátima as its own national shrine with a huge basilica. During the Spanish civil war the Fátima message became strongly anti-communist and was annexed to the dictator's panoply of political symbolism with the slogan 'Fátima for religion, *Fado* songs for nostalgia, and Football for the glory of Portugal.' In the 1950s Fátima was a rendezvous for some of the world's most reactionary statesmen and in the 1960s Salazar had the supreme satisfaction of welcoming the pope there, to the immense dismay of liberal Catholics around the world. The coincidence of state and church interests was not complete and Salazar surprised the bishops by abolishing his own Catholic party along with all other political movements when in 1932 he crafted his dictatorial constitution. His parricidal bluntness even extended to the cardinal, his old flatmate, who was kept at arm's length to ensure political supremacy. When relations with the Vatican were restored by the concordat of 1940 the separation of church and state was formally preserved.

Salazar's attitude to the monarchists was equally cautious in that he needed their support but did not want to concede too much influence to them. When the exiled king died in 1932, however, he lost no time in consolidating his position and promoted himself from minister of finance and the colonies to the chairmanship of the cabinet. In so doing he liberated himself from the residual military umpires who had hitherto presided over his governments though he took great care to give close attention to satisfying the social and financial aspirations of the military who, having put him in power, still had the guns to remove him again should he neglect their self-esteem.

While priests, monarchists and soldiers were shrewdly incorporated into the élite which underpinned Salazar's authority, the illiterate majority were kept firmly in ignorance, not only as a policy of monetarist saving, but also as a form of social control. Nominally children were sent to school for four years but in practice schools were often remote or unavailable and child labour could not be released from the struggling farms. Education was the escape route for the few who made up the rock of salazarian support and who were primed to believe in the myth of Portuguese passivity that was propagated to foreigners and made peasants resemble the 'good nigger' of America or the 'happy native' of South Africa. The grotesque obscurantism of the propaganda put out by petty rulers was espied in 1936 by Gonzague de Reynold.

A LIÇÃO DE SALAZAR

DEUS, PÁTRIA, FAMÍLIA:
A TRILOGIA
DA EDUCAÇÃO NACIONAL

41   Gender stereotypes and class deference were instilled into
Salazar's 'poor but pious' peasants both by propaganda and by
the infiltration of secret police informers who denounced any
independence of mind.

The Portuguese peasant is religious and will remain so despite the ravages
caused in his mind by the scandalous anti-clerical republic. On the other
hand he is superstitious with a superstition which survives from an old
paganism sometimes related to devil worship. He is sober when he has not
too much money to spend, and he lives simply with few wants. With the
exception of a few large landowners he is poor but does not complain. The
Portuguese peasant has an air of contentment, if not of happiness, which it
is a pleasure to behold. He is extremely easy to govern.
    Cited in Jacques Georgel, *Le Salazarisme: Histoire et Bilan 1926–1974*
                                        (Paris, 1981) p. 82, translated.

The 'easy government' of the Portuguese was achieved in the 1930s
by means of an all-pervasive political police similar to, if not trained
by, the German Gestapo. The political police was not a large force
and never rose much above 2,000 fully enrolled staff though it probably had 10,000 part-time informers planted in every hamlet or
institution. It was above the law and the government and was an-
swerable to Salazar alone until the day he suffered a stroke in 1968
when it was the police chief, and not the state president or the army

commander, who sat at his bedside deciding how to fill the power
vacuum. Cultivated rumours about the secret police's use of torture, detention and even assassination increased its effectiveness as
a means of suppressing political discussion at home and later disseminating fear in the colonies too. Salazar justified 'a few cuffs to
make terrorists confess, and so save innocent lives' but fear became
a well-honed weapon in his hands and passers-by on the street in
front of police headquarters were allowed to hear the screams of
detainees subjected to both bluntly crude and exquisitely refined
forms of torture. Portugal did not kill 'surplus' people in the Soviet
or Nazi style in the 1930s, nor did it suffer the carnage of Spain, but
disloyalty to the leader and any questioning of the inequitable social order was repressed as subversion or communism. The essential
complement to this effective political police was an efficient censorship. Nothing could be published or broadcast without careful and
costly scrutiny. Anything that might alarm public opinion or dispar-
age the dignity of the nation was cut from newspaper proofs and
replaced with approved material. Government stories were carried
as though they were editorial copy, and even the sporting press was
checked for any lack of patriotic hyperbole.

While the German-style political police relieved the army muti-
neers of 1926 of their responsibility for 'cleansing' the country of
'demagogues' a French-style gendarmerie inherited from the republic was given responsibility for keeping 'law and order'. Old soldiers
were given the status they craved but were exonerated from responsibilities which had highlighted their incompetence and were not again
put to the test until 1961. Officers preened themselves vainly and
lorded it over illiterate conscripts who, the cynics claimed, resembled
the armies of Louis XIV rather than those of Hitler. The lifestyle of
officers, however, was carefully ordered by clever social engineering
and they could only marry Catholic wives with school qualifica-
tions or personal fortunes to ensure their harmonious integration
into the dominant moneyed and educated élite. The requirement of
church weddings for officers alienated some otherwise conservative
soldiers including the redoubtable Norton de Matos who had served
as minister of war in 1916–17, had been the republic's high com-
missioner in Angola and had served as grandmaster of the outlawed

freemasons. He was Salazar's most tenacious political rival and had the Catholic-led politicians failed to sustain the conservative consensus Norton de Matos would probably have been the focus for a masonic-led coalition of military and civilian interests. In 1948 Norton de Matos tried to stand for election as president but even under a tightly restricted franchise political liberties were a fraud and he abandoned the attempt.

The militarisation of Portugal was not limited to soldiers and policemen. A regimented youth movement wore Salazar uniforms stamped with the letter 'S' and were commanded by a law lecturer Marcelo Caetano who eventually succeeded Salazar as prime minister. Only the most wealthy and privileged of youths could escape the discipline of the brigades. The adult counterpart of the youth brigades was the Portuguese Legion which wore green shirts and was called upon to defend public order. It was especially active at times when the government had to assure foreign observers of its 'respectability' by holding 'elections'. Elections raised destabilising expectations even when the only permissible voters were well enough educated and sufficiently affluent that they could be expected to be grateful to the government. The Legion was not a fascist paramilitary movement, nor was it a single party like the 'National Union' which Salazar had built up around himself despite the abolition of political parties, but it gave the government the necessary muscle to deal with the 86 per cent of the population who were politically voiceless. It was also a force that could be used to show solidarity with the Spanish 'nationalists' when they attacked their own democratic republic in 1936.

Acceptance of 'stability at a price' was one of the keys to the longevity of the Portuguese dictatorship. Inflation had hurt investors and Salazar's determination to maintain a hard currency based on old-fashioned gold provided a certainty that had been missing under the republic. The emphasis on national pride was also effective in broadening the basis of consent for the dictatorship. The new state boasted of its power with heavy architectural projects. Public buildings with façades of neo-classical decor representing social order were built by the unemployed labourers of the recession thus minimising their susceptibility to communist 'agitation'. Architects short of commissions were willing to abandon their modernism and help the state implant itself on the landscape rather than be consigned to professional oblivion. Massive residential blocks were erected on prestigious sites in the capital and the technical university was given elaborate new premises. Historical monuments were built to commemorate the glory of Portugal and the power of its former dictators, especially Pombal. The last great memorial was built in white stone at the mouth of the Tagus to celebrate the fifth centenary of the regime's most heroic ancestor-myth, Henry the Navigator.

In 1930 Salazar was in charge of the ministry of colonies when, after the collapse of Wall Street, the empire suddenly became of much greater potential economic importance than hitherto. Before that Brazil had continued to dominate the overseas dimensions of Portuguese affairs, buying exports, receiving immigrants and sending back the small savings of a million exiled peasants. In 1930 the doors were closed not only to Brazil, but also to the United States where large communities of economic refugees were being firmly established in both New England and California. Since trade with Europe, including Britain, was also in recession it suddenly became urgent to replace the informal empire in the Americas with new overseas outlets for people and goods. The only option seemed to be Africa and Salazar set about devising a new colonial pact. His aim was to terminate the indirect colonialism of foreign-dominated chartered companies and establish a new economic nationalism more favourable to Portugal itself. The ideology, however, was tempered with pragmatism. In southern Mozambique the treaty with South Africa to supply contract workers for the mines in return for payments in gold was reconfirmed. In central Mozambique the British-dominated company which governed the province and ran the harbours, railways and postal services to Rhodesia was allowed to retain its licence until the expiry date in 1940 but thereafter alien sovereignty was terminated. A more delicate aspect of foreign influence involved the presence of foreign missionary societies which provided health and education in the colonies but were constantly suspected of undermining the patriotic loyalty expected of colonial subjects. Although Protestant missionaries were offensive to the new nationalism it was not deemed wise to terminate their rights which had been enshrined in the diplomacy which had given Portugal its imperial territories during the Victorian partition of Africa. Pragmatism had to prevail as Salazar sought new ways of extracting colonial wealth from the African continent.

The first economic drive attempted in the colonies was in the field of cotton cultivation. The recession had cut off the dollar remittances of migrants and Portugal could no longer easily afford to buy United States cotton. It tried to make do with colonial cotton instead. The textile mills protested that colonial cotton had poorer quality, shorter fibres and dearer prices than American cotton but they were compelled to buy it anyway as a means of saving on foreign exchange and of subsidising the development of the new empire. The African peasants protested too, saying that cotton growing gave a poorer level of subsistence than planting domestic food crops. The state insisted, however, and farmers in both Angola and Mozambique were issued with seed which they were compelled to plant on their own land and with their own hands regardless of the risk from uncertain climatic conditions and the poor prospect of being paid a viable price for their crop by state-controlled buying agencies. By shifting the risks of cotton growing from the white commercial colonists to the black subject peasants the colonial state engendered a sharp political confrontation. In 1945 famine led to rebellion in the cotton fields of Angola. Salazar and his then colonial minister, Caetano, investigated the uprising and reported that the famine had been nothing but a figment of the imagination of the 'natives' whose idleness was well known. Colonial officers understood the crisis better but were peremptorily silenced until the next cotton-belt famine broke out in 1961 and began the revolutionary process which eventually destroyed the whole Portuguese empire. Before that happened, however, Portugal tried much more successful ways of transferring wealth from Africa to Europe.

Until 1930 the most visible migrants from Portugal to Angola were convicts who could be seen weeding the roads of Luanda city wearing their prison chains. Salazar ended the convict image of the colonies, though Africans continued to work in chain gangs for another thirty years, and encouraged free men to go to Africa in search of economic survival. The immigrants were reluctant, illiterate and racist. They spread out into the backlands as petty shopkeepers, siring large families on their defenceless black servant-girls and buying maize and coffee from peasant families in exchange for usurious credit and ruinous wine. The most successful money lenders bought land from defaulting clients and imported forced migrant labour from the remote districts to work it. The migrants were paid in tokens that could only be redeemed for expensive loin cloths and grog in the farm shop. The crops were headloaded to the nearest colonial railway by porters when lorries and petrol were scarce. Maize, together with dried fish from the South Atlantic, was sold to the industrial belt of the Belgian Congo and coffee was exported to America to rebuild Lisbon's dollar reserves. On the east coast plantation companies took over peasant coconut groves and turned their owners into wage labourers while forced migrants from the hinterland were recruited to plant sisal and sugar. The colonial system was makeshift but effective and by the 1950s Salazar had ensured that a high proportion of all colonial subjects were unwillingly 'working for Portugal'.

The empire expected to find mineral wealth with which to finance a programme of industrialisation back in Portugal, but the winnings were sparse compared to those of South Africa or the Belgian Congo. In 1917 diamonds had been located in a not yet fully conquered corner of Angola and a concession was granted to a company which had links with the De Beers diamond trading cartel and which established an almost autonomous mining state within the colonial state. In Mozambique enough coal was mined by a South African concessionaire to keep the steam trains running but all the gold seams of the region were on the British side of the Rhodesian border. After the Second World War foreign concessionaires were given a railway in south Angola to extract iron ore but the project missed the temporary boom in iron prices. The great transformation came only after 1954 with the discovery of deep-sea oil in the Cabinda enclave north of Angola. Salazar was ambivalent about the discovery of oil. The petroleum industry was even less amenable to national control than other mineral industries and foreign capital backed by foreign politics was the only way of realising the potential. Eventually the wells were opened, and a somewhat ghostly refinery was built on a new industrial site in southern Portugal in the hope of processing the oil, but Cabinda remained firmly under the control of Gulf Oil not only during the last days of the empire but also throughout the struggles for the control of independent Angola.

The first steps towards change in Salazar's enclosed imperial world began in 1943. In Italy Mussolini fell, in Spain Franco continued to refuse to repay his civil war debts to Germany by joining the Axis, in North Africa western Muslims came under the sway of American invaders and in the Middle East the British consolidated their hold on the oil lanes of eastern Muslims. In Lisbon Rose Macaulay arrived from the British ministry of information to explore the rival sympathies of the Portuguese towards Hitler and Churchill. She reported with impeccable scholarly caution that she found it hard to believe that many people were genuinely pro-German though she admired the ragged news vendors scampering over the hot cobbles who seemed to know unerringly to whom to offer *Das Reich* and which customers would prefer the *Daily Express*. There was nevertheless great astonishment among the German community and their middle-class admirers when Salazar was compelled to bend his neutrality and grant Britain military access to the Azores Islands. There was equal astonishment among the British community and its associates two years later when he mourned the death of Hitler by flying Portugal's flags at half-mast. From then onwards the world around changed rapidly: Britain was defeated at Suez in 1956 and decided to abandon its colonies in Africa, even going so far as to send its prime minister to South Africa in 1960 to warn the white nationalists that a transfer of power to the black majority was inevitable. His message was rejected in Cape Town, but was unexpectedly received loud and clear in Angola and Mozambique where a rebellion broke out which woke Portuguese high society from its complacency in a way that the European war had failed to do.

Political unease at home preceded the outbreak of the colonial wars by a few years. Portugal had been admitted to the United Nations in 1955 in spite of a poor democratic record because it was both white and anti-communist and could therefore be expected to vote with Washington's Latin American client republics and Britain's white Commonwealth. In 1958 evidence of democratic progress was being sought by Portugal's western supporters and a presidential election was held. The government fielded an insignificant admiral to replace an outgoing president who had shown disquieting signs of independent judgement. The opposition on the other hand managed to find a general with impeccable army credentials as its standard bearer. In 1943 it had been General Delgado who had renegotiated Portugal's alliance with Britain. Now as a presidential candidate he announced, through the small window in the censorship which an election permitted, that if elected he would dismiss Salazar. The well-to-do middle classes who were allowed to vote showed unanticipated enthusiasm for change after thirty years of glacial national austerity. The ballot had to be rigged and the bold general was driven into exile and denounced with such paranoia by Salazar that the secret police finally decided to lure him to a fictional meeting of conspirators in Spain and assassinate him. The failure of a senior general to tame the dictatorship aroused new political aspirations in the army and in 1962 junior officers attempted an inept and abortive *coup d'état*. By then, however, their seniors had found a new role defending the empire from subversion and aggression.

After living comfortably off Salazar's generous pension for thirty years the army's return to active duty got off to a bad start. In China Salazar recognised that the forces of nationalism were not to be trifled with and came to a pragmatic agreement with the communist government of 1950 over the miniature colony of Macau. This enabled the enclave to flourish on finance and gambling under a quasi-colonial administration and permitted Salazar to think that he ruled an empire on which the sun hardly ever set. In India, by contrast, the confrontation with nationalism was more severe and a colonial war led to an instant defeat which left Portugal licking its wounds. It expressed injured innocence when Nehru abandoned his morally reputable demand that Goa be given democracy to invade and annex the Portuguese colonial enclaves. The Portuguese rout revealed the gap between the government, which ordered resistance to the death, and the soldiers, who surrendered instantly against the overwhelming Indian forces. More comically the fiasco was also alleged to reveal the inexperience of the general staff which, when asked to send sausages to Goa, sent pork ones quite forgetting that its own code word for cannon shells was 'sausages'. Portugal's premier colony thus succumbed amid recrimination and farce rather than in bloodshed. In Africa the colonial war was to be an altogether more gruesome and protracted affair.

When war broke out in Africa there were sound economic as well as patriotic reasons for suppressing the rebellion. Angolan colonists in particular had thrived ever since the commodity boom of the Korean War. The rapidly expanding coffee plantations became the basis of a new prosperity which was transferred to the towns of Portugal where colonial speculators built small blocks of high-rise flats with precarious wooden scaffolding. In the 1950s a new generation of migrants, including wives and families, doubled the settler population of Portuguese Africa and created a captive colonial market for Portuguese wines and textiles as well as for the new consumer goods of the reviving post-war economy. Following the old hypocritical tradition of 'pleasing the British', and incidentally adopting a former French tropical practice, the African territories were cosmetically renamed 'overseas provinces' and were deemed to be integral parts of Portugal and not colonies subject to international supervision. The settlers, however, behaved like colonisers, reformed nothing, and triggered off the African rebellion of 1961 in Angola. They then organised vigilante commandos to resist African claims to independence. Their murderous efforts, however, were not enough to crush the anti-colonial protests of despair and large expeditionary armies had to be sent first to Angola and then to Guinea and Mozambique in order to hold the empire for another decade.

In 1963 the colonial war brought more dramatic changes to Portugal's social culture than the world war had brought in 1943. The ultra-conservative social traditions of the 'grande bourgeoisie' were gradually eased after surviving both world wars in Edwardian isolation and splendour. The abundance of very cheap labour was eroded by emigration to the colonies in the 1950s and by army conscription, or the flight from conscription, in the 1960s. Although domestic service became less lavishly available ladies' maids continued to work a sixteen-hour day in private homes and uniformed male children jumped to attention to open hotel doors. The government proclaimed its social modernity by discontinuing the registration of common bawds and by ending the public health licensing of the parlours, complete with string quartets, in which young ladies

42   Portuguese conscripts and African army recruits with
weapons captured from the liberation forces during the colonial wars of 1961–74.

catered for the private sexual tastes of salazarian high society. Plebeian pleasures, however, continued to be taken in charabanc rides
to the beach, and all-concealing costumes remained *de rigueur* for
men as well as women. Despite the beginnings of social change tram
conductors continued to earn the equivalent of one pound sterling a
week while selling penny tickets to the leisured classes riding home
late from the opera. Workers got no welfare or pension from the
primitive but over-staffed state and many still got no education
either. To some of these drones the army might have seemed like
a welcome adventure. To others the threat of four dangerous years
in the African forests was the spur they needed to escape from their
treadmill and flee to France. By the end of the decade a million
Portuguese were working in mainland Europe alongside Algerians
and Turks. Their hours were still long but they were liberated from
the oppressiveness of hierarchical order and returned home partially freed from the reflex compulsion to touch their forelocks in

43 In the 1960s almost as many Portuguese lived in the shanty slums of Paris and elsewhere in France as in all the Portuguese colonies combined.

deference to the gentry. They were also imbued with new cultural and economic expectations.

Provincial Portugal suffered particularly bitterly from the colonial wars. Whereas educated city men might expect to become non-commissioned officers and to pursue a career on the side in Africa, rural conscripts from northern villages, where illiterate artisans still head-loaded their wares to the nearest motor road, could expect nothing but alternating boredom and danger in Africa. When they left the village more work than ever fell on the shoulders of women. Life was hard and lonely and many forsaken sweethearts either remained spinsters in a world where men became scarce or crossed the mountains with the draft dodgers to find work in France. When the

French labour market became saturated they moved on to Belgium, Germany and Switzerland gaining a new vision of the outside world and its opportunities. The successful migrants put their savings into two forms of prestige expenditure, a motor car which those who were not considered outlaws proudly drove home each holiday to park by the village pump in full view of their jealous neighbours, and a concrete house pieced together summer by summer on the family plot. Once the roof was on the dream house stereos, washing-machines, television sets and refrigerators were brought back from 'Europe' in anticipation of the arrival in the village of the electricity grid. Prestige spending by migrants was probably not a great force for change in the north any more than Brazilian migration had been in the nineteenth century. Instead the postal orders sent home from France to peasant mothers preserved the rural economy with its small plots, its meagre livestock and its tradition of giving alms to the parish church.

The lot of northern women, whether peasants on the land or domestic servants in France, could not have been more sharply contrasted with that of emancipated urban women. Middle-class daughters went to university, travelled by air and gained interesting jobs in the colonies. Chaperones were dispensed with in the wide-open frontier societies of Africa and domestic drudgery was performed by black country girls. Riding to tropical beaches on the back of an expensive motor-scooter entailed a freedom quite different from being formally escorted to the Lisbon bull-ring by an approved beau tailed by a duenna. Excitement was enhanced for women as well as men by a national passion for football which transcended class boundaries as Benfica replaced Real Madrid to become Europe's favourite soccer team of the 1960s. Emancipated students, and especially women students, even began daringly to talk of politics and fantasise about forbidden ideologies, though with little personal experience of the meaning of deprivation or oppression. When the revolution came this gilded youth was out on the streets, drunk with excitement in its temporary solidarity with the industrial workers.

Social change was brought to Portuguese society not only by migration to France and Africa but even more pervasively by industrialisation at home. The idyllic and timeless Arcadia to which Salazar consigned the Portuguese in his imagination could not finance a major war to hold on to his colonial empire. In a fit of unexpected flexibility his political entourage therefore turned to the United States in search of economic modernisation. America, after entering the Azores airbases on British coat-tails in 1943, had supported Portugal steadily, allowing the regime to survive the fall of the dictators in 1945, then bringing it into the NATO alliance, and most dramatically permitting it to retain its colonies after the Angolan rebellion of 1961. In return the Portuguese moderated their economic nationalism and opened both the homeland and the colonies to new foreign investment. At the same time a new generation of Portuguese entrepreneurs, encouraged by the great banking families, gave domestic investment in services and manufacturing industries a sudden burst of growth. Textiles, brewing, electronics, plastics, construction materials, food processing, domestic goods all expanded their production in the partially liberated political climate and created a miniature consumer society impatient with the old social constraints. At the same time the old heavy metal workers of the shipyards began to flex their muscles though they did not officially regain the right to strike which they had lost when the republic foundered in 1926.

The industrial burst of the last years of the dictatorship resembled the industrial burst in the last years of the monarchy. It was dramatic by the past standards of Portugal, but it still left the country behind its rivals. Monarchical industrialisation in the nineteenth century had achieved a growth rate of 3 per cent but that did not match the 8 per cent scored by Tsarist Russia. Under the salazarian economic revival clothing and fabrics replaced cork and wood-pulp in the export league in 1960 and soon afterwards textiles overtook food and farm produce as well. By the 1970s machinery and chemicals exceeded agricultural exports, and yet Portuguese levels of wealth remained stubbornly below those of 'fascist' Spain. The limits to industrial growth were matched by the limits of industrial ownership. Ten great families owned 168 firms and controlled 53 per cent of the national wealth, while a mere 1 per cent of the Portuguese population was deemed to belong to the select few which the social order maintained in style. Although industrial ownership was concentrated, industrial production was diffuse and even in the 1980s, after a revolution and a wide-scale programme of nationalisation,

98.5 per cent of firms still employed fewer than 500 workers and an overwhelming majority had fewer than 50. Even on this limited scale, however, the building of shoe factories and sugar refineries, of metal workshops and flour mills, brought great changes to communities which still struggled to carry their corn up the hill to the windmill and took their boots to be repaired year in year out by the cobbler on the corner.

The creeping social change which industry brought to Portugal was paralleled by a much more visible social change of the 1960s brought on by the advent of the package tourist industry. The rise in north European prosperity and the accompanying search for south European sunshine brought a severe challenge to the social conservatism that had been imposed on Portugal. The elect had always been welcome to visit Portugal in style and a minor colony of former kings and courtiers held balls in Estoril at which the cream of local society brought out their daughters. Holiday-making by the *hoi polloi*, however, was quite another matter. Mass tourism was a fast way of earning hard currency but it brought material aspirations to the 'docile' workers who had formerly been so 'easy to govern'. New music, new dress, new affluence, new leisure, new hairstyles, new moralities, were all a threat to a closed society. And yet Portugal had few resources as potentially marketable as its untouched beaches and eventually the old kingdom of the Algarve was opened up by a bridge across the Lisbon river, an improved motor road, an airport runway and the foreign development of hotels. The new sun belt could not remain a foreign enclave and Portuguese speculators and holiday-makers followed the trail. When the African empire collapsed in 1974 colonial innkeepers put their frustrated energies into tourist enterprises. Their liberated colonial mores were more in tune with those of the tourists, whom they simultaneously mocked and envied, than were those of the staid local population. The hoteliers exploited their clients as hard as they could without driving them back to the Costa Brava or onward to the tropical islands of the tourist diaspora. The middle-class vacationers down from Lisbon aped the foreign ways and brought the revolutionary pressure for social liberation one step forward.

The church was slow to accept the transformation of society that caught up with Portugal in the 1960s. Although many people in the south were covertly communist and anti-clerical, in the north religious processions were still performed on holy days and the magical powers of Fátima continued to hold sway. Pope John XXIII and the reforms of the second Vatican Council caused a frisson of horror throughout most of the Portuguese church hierarchy and his premature death in 1963 was greeted with undisguised relief. Latin American concepts of 'liberation theology' were not welcomed in Portugal, though the bishop of Oporto tried to interest the church in social responsibility and was exiled for his pains. In Mozambique an even more radical bishop, Dom Sebastião Soares de Resende, bishop of Beira, stepped out of line and was reviled for failing to support the propaganda of the empire. The relationship of church and empire was a difficult one. The Portuguese church had rarely been very active in the mission field but had concentrated on providing parish services for settlers and left the converting and nurturing of black subject races to foreign priests or to Protestants. Italian, Dutch and Spanish priests found themselves uncomfortably caught trying to defend the welfare of their African parishioners against the increasingly aggressive repression of the colonial state during the wars of liberation. Portuguese churchmen who sympathised with the 'disloyal' accusations of racial exploitation and oppression were singled out for particular vilification. It was the church's condemnation of the dictatorship in the tropics that beamed a foreign spotlight on Portugal and brought the revolution to a head.

The African wars had a profound effect on Portugal. First of all they gave the government a new lease of life and then, in 1974, they brought it toppling down after forty-eight years of continuity. The new lease of life was achieved by a political astuteness that might not have been expected of an ageing regime. First of all Portugal forced the United States to undertake a volte-face in its African policy and instead of supporting the rise of a black national bourgeoisie and emancipation from colonial tutelage, as it had insistently done in British, French and Belgian colonies, the USA gave Portugal a licence to reconquer its African possessions. In exchange for a renewal of the military lease on the airbase of the Azores, America discreetly allowed military equipment designed for the defence of the North Atlantic to be diverted for use in colonial expeditions.

The army was re-equipped and given the budgetary resources to fight a major war while its officers were promoted and given opportunities to make private fortunes on the side while serving in the colonies. The officer corps was particularly sweetened by its control of the black market in currency which enabled a brigadier to build a high-rise apartment block after each tour of duty in Africa. The colonial rebels, by contrast, were so ferociously dragooned by the invading colonial army that thousands of people were killed in Angola alone and many more joined the columns of refugees who fled to Zaire, almost depopulating the northern provinces of the colony but leaving pockets of insurgents which kept the army employed, if not stretched, for the next thirteen years. The biggest military task was patrolling the open savannahs of eastern Angola which were infiltrated by guerrilla movements based in havens of exile. Increasingly the patrols were carried out by black conscripts paid to defend the colony against their own kith and kin.

In addition to restoring the pride of the army, Africa stimulated the Portuguese economy. A quarter of a million expatriates and settler in Angola and half that number in Mozambique built up service industries and processing plants such as few other tropical colonies had seen. The construction industry thrived, tourism reached the Indian Ocean resorts, aerial survey plotted out new cattle ranches, huge hydroelectric projects were built, white peasants irrigated rice paddies, factory trawlers froze fish, the wells pumped oil, the breweries multiplied their output and the empire produced a quarter of a million tons of coffee a year sold for American dollars and good Dutch guilders. In the 1960s the bubble showed no signs of bursting and in 1968 the management of Portugal and the empire passed from Salazar to Caetano with barely a hiccup. The old man lived on despite a crippling stroke and his policies survived. The army insisted that his successor should be a civilian so as to keep its own political role invisible. The appointed heir worried the admiral-president when he appeared to signal that he wanted to turn left but he actually carried on as before with if anything a tightening of the controls over public freedom and only cosmetic changes to the institutions. Change, however, was only postponed and in the 1970s a minor recession in settler prosperity coincided with the revitalisation of African nationalism, this time not in Angola but in Mozambique.

In the late 1960s the liberation movement in Mozambique suffered two severe blows when its 'liberated zones' in the northern provinces were partially recaptured by the colonial army and its president, Eduardo Mondlane, was assassinated by a parcel bomb sent to his office. A new military leader, Samora Machel, was chosen and a new strategy was adopted which aimed to attack the settler heartlands of Mozambique, disrupt the railway to Rhodesia and prevent the completion of the Zambezi dam which was intended to supply South Africa with cheap electricity and so ensure that South Africa and its European partners would help Portugal to protect Mozambique from black liberators. The new African nationalist strategy was partially successful. Although work on the dam was not delayed, the guerrillas did cross the river and disrupt communications and production in central Mozambique. The colonial security forces felt humiliated and adopted terrorist tactics learnt from Vietnam to burn down villages and round up peasants in security compounds. The missionaries publicised the massacres and documented the excavation of mass graves. The army began to wonder whether colonial wars were good for its image after all.

The most public questioning of colonial continuity after the death of Salazar came from a monocled cavalry general called Spínola who had been commander-in-chief in Portugal's third African war fought in Guinea. He became convinced that his army could not win against the committed ideology of irregular forces seeking to liberate their homeland. Some of his officers had even come to admire the political thoughts of their opponents and although the Guinea leader, like the Mozambique one, had been assassinated his writings on political liberation in a poor agrarian country were seen to have relevance to Portugal itself. The ideological questioning by left-wing officers in Guinea, and the declining morale of defeated officers in Mozambique, struck a chord with trade-union-minded officers in Portugal itself. The captains saw their careers in Africa being undermined by highly educated conscripts who were ruining their chances of promotion to the lucrative opportunities of their seniors. When, in February 1974, Spínola published a book cautiously asking whether a commonwealth-type community might not provide a better future for the Portuguese empire than another generation of warfare, junior officers heard the message. They organised political meetings where they plotted their coup out in the countryside beyond the ears of police surveillance devices. Before dawn on 25 April 1974 a radio station played a song about 'the land of the fraternity' and columns of tanks rolled into Lisbon to be greeted with carnations by delirious crowds. President Tomás and his prime minister Caetano were quickly dispatched to Brazil and General Spínola became the improbable mascot of his Marxist juniors. For the next year and a half the April revolution unfolded dramatically before being arrested by a counter-coup and then replaced by a democratic regime under light military supervision.

7

Democracy and the European Community

The April revolution of 1974 brought a ray of happiness to Portugal and dispelled the melancholia which had been its social hallmark for so long. The mournful *fado* songs were confined to tourist spots and the liberated generation threw itself into twentieth-century beat music. The Lisbon book fair flooded Avenida da Liberdade with ideas that had previously been available only under the counter, and publishing houses translated instant paperbacks on such forbidden subjects as psychology and social history as well as disseminating Marxism and modern fiction. The communist party organised enormous summer festivals to which the most famous of the world's musical groups were invited and huge crowds spent balmy nights wandering among the hundreds of acres of stalls eating, drinking, listening and fearlessly fraternising. In the euphoria there was little room for recrimination and persecution though a few secret policemen were exposed and incarcerated and some successful members of the business community found it expedient to follow a handful of politicians into temporary exile in Brazil. The soldiers found it as difficult as their predecessors had in 1926 to achieve a stable form of government and a few aspired to replace the monetarist certainties of the old order with new Marxist certainties.

The communists were the first people to claim the revolution as their own. They, almost alone, had survived as a clandestine political force throughout the dictatorship. Unlike the communists of mainland Europe, however, they had not shed their hard-line heritage to court democratic popularity rather than Marxist purity.

44   The young officers who took over the streets of Lisbon on 25 April 1974 without firing a shot also became radical advocates of the large-scale expropriation of rural estate farms.

Their heroic silver-haired leader, Cunhal, had escaped from prison in 1960 and fled to exile in Moscow. He returned to a tumultuous welcome, but maintained an autocratic control over his party which did not endorse even the mild Soviet reforms of the Khrushchev era let alone the Euro-communism of the west. The hard line did not attract the left-wing intellectuals any more than it attracted the democratic socialists, and it was an anathema to the Catholic provinces of the north. The communist vote fluctuated around one-eighth of the electorate concentrated in two main regions of the country. The first focus of communist mobilisation was the industrial zone facing Lisbon where trade unionism was restored to the workforce with angry urgency. The other communist enclave was on the great southern farms where Catholicism had always been weak and hardly any priests led a peasant resistance to atheistic ideologies. It was in the south that farm labourers remembered an old political proposal drawn up by the republic fifty years before to transfer the control of land from absentee landlords to working labourers.

'Agrarian reform' became one of the most dynamic issues of the April revolution but also one of the most contentious. In the towns industrialists, bankers and shareholders temporarily fled the country to await the outcome of the social upheavals, or even to settle permanently in the more conservative financial climate of Brazil, but on the land the question of common ownership and nationalisation was fought over in a long struggle. While political splinter groups marched up and down the avenues of Lisbon devising slogans and wielding cans of red paint, the key reform of property ownership was determined in the Alentejo province far beyond the river. For a brief period the radical army captains of the revolution entrusted the communist party with control of the ministry of agriculture. It genuinely tried to improve the lot of farmers on the southern estates, but it had no understanding of rural society. A socialist minister of agriculture who subsequently tried to ride the storm of the agrarian reform the communists had unleashed remembered the year 1975 in these loosely translated terms:

Throughout two years of reform aspirations had no limits and the possible was never a defined quantity. 'Moderation' was always equated with a restoration of the old order, and the distinction between liberty and revenge was eroded. Shades of difference between equality and tyranny were dimmed. Everything was questioned, social hierarchy and atavistic oppression, human rights and common lawfulness. In the social turbulence the struggle for power overwhelmed the struggle for liberty even among those who had previously had no liberty. As in all revolutions justice rubbed shoulders with injustice. Social and political action became more extreme, each victory pointing the way to another conquest. Finally, in 1977, a point of crystallisation, of equilibrium, was achieved with advances, retreats and compromises, but whether or not the balance would be stable was not yet predictable. The rural wage earners of the Alentejo won some rights and privileges while the owners of the land and of the irrigation waters lost some. Small and medium farmers won little, or even lost in status. The revolution created rights and destroyed oppression but revolutionary logic did not always respect justice.

António Barreto, *Memória da Reforma Agrária*, (Publicações
Europa-America, Lisbon) no date, vol. I, p. 14.

The mythology of Marxist revolutionary theory places peasants and workers shoulder to shoulder as allies. In the great plains of Portugal they were opponents in the struggle for agrarian reform. Peasants had gained little from the nominally 'corporative' salazarian state which had given no support to entrepreneurs on the smallest of scales. Communism saw farmers on whatever scale as 'bosses' who exploited their workers. Thus in the conflict between landowners and landworkers peasants and tenant farmers were disowned by both sides and painfully squeezed. One such farmer in the anonymous crowd recorded his childhood, walking eleven kilometres to school barefoot with a fertiliser bag as a cape, becoming the teacher of his fellows at the age of eleven when the schoolmistress became pregnant, staving off famine in the late 1940s by gleaning fallen bits of cork along the roadside knowing that if caught there would be a thrashing at the police station, planting paddy rice alongside his elderly tenant father to dissuade the landowner from terminating the tenancy, then prospering in the 1960s when labour was scarce. By the 1970s he was renting his own land, buying his own tractors, hiring his own workforce of twenty-five men when suddenly, in October 1975, he was evicted as a capitalist, an exploiter. 'Workers' from the city led by 'soldiers' and 'graduates' invaded his farm in the name of revolution and reform and he was officially dispossessed. Eighteen months later, when the counter-revolution took effect, the police helped him recover his tenancy though not without acrimony.

The land reform programme adopted slogans too coarse to recognise that for some people economic pressures had already begun to improve working conditions. When labour was scarce it was difficult to expect men to work from dawn to dusk and the 48-hour week had made its debut before the revolution. Wages improved and some estate managers adopted paternalistic measures to hold their best workers or to attract them back when they had finished their army service. At the same time farm workers could be suspicious of trade union demands for shorter hours, fearing that if guaranteed an eight-hour day 'they would go hungry for four hours a day'. Despite the beginnings of change exploitation did survive and some southern labourers welcomed the revolutionary policy of turning large estates, or groups of estates, into collective units of production. The new collective farms imposed by the soldiers from the city did not flourish, however, and experienced labourers were all too often replaced by inexperienced ones with poor work records and no incentives. On some collective farms management began well and patterns of worker consultation were effectively established. At the same time state agencies provided capital for investment and mechanisation. But prudence diminished as credit grew and in 1976 the second season's harvests showed poor promise. A socialist government was forced to bite the bullet and incur the wrath of communists and their sympathisers by reversing the programme of collectivisation and inviting back at least the working farmers if not the absentee landlords. Many labourers returned to their old farms for security and accepted that the great rise in wages would not keep pace with inflation. The ideologically enthused soldiers were demobilised and vanished and the old republican gendarmerie returned to police duty in defence of private property.

Another experiment in common ownership took place in the towns where the governments of transition undertook a wide-ranging programme of nationalisation. This programme caused as great, if not greater, political controversy than land reform. The original hero of the April revolution, the monocled General Spínola, had close contact with the great industrial families of Portugal. When he had tried to modernise the colonial system in Guinea by giving economic satisfaction to the African population he had persuaded his friends in the Melo family, which controlled the largest of the nation's industrial complexes and owned extensive colonial investments, to support his experiment. When the revolution broke out in Portugal itself Spínola was able to ensure that industrial policy was initially moderate and for some months the interests of the great financiers were effectively defended by their associates among the generals. Soon, however, the more radical voices of the army captains and the trade union leaders began to be heard. Spínola tried to quieten them by calling on the 'silent majority' in September 1974 to march in protest against the rising prospect of 'anarchy' and union power. His experiment in right-wing populism failed and he resigned as president. He next planned a *coup d'état*, to be launched on 11 March 1975, but failed again and fled temporarily to Spain. After this renewed right-wing threat the left-wing army captains of the April rebellion, now calling themselves 'the armed forces movement', increased their hold on government. A series of communist-inspired nationalisations was adopted which went far beyond the initial state control of the privately owned monopolies that supplied such services as water and electricity.

The most obvious target for expropriation in the interests of its workers and of society at large was the Melo business empire which

45   Mário Soares was a persecuted democrat under the dictatorship, a flexible democratic socialist after the revolution of 1974 and a paternal president of the second republic from 1986 to 1996.

Spínola had tried so hard to defend. It was the largest financial complex in the Iberian peninsula and held 10 per cent of all share capital in the whole of Portugal. Other family-based networks which virtually monopolised banking and insurance were nationalised with due legal process. The financial barons had also controlled the press which thus fell into government hands, though attempts to use it for propaganda purposes had little effect on rural peoples who were predominantly illiterate or on urban readers long accustomed to mendacity in their newspapers. State control went further as the revolution reached its summer climax in 1975 and spread to petroleum refining, steel rolling, tobacco packing, beer brewing, fertiliser manufacturing, shipbuilding, pharmaceutical supplying, not to mention the provision of transport by road, rail and air. About 20 per cent of Portuguese industry came to be either government owned or government managed. The old middle class so feared the rise of state power that as many as 10,000 property owners and shareholders departed for Brazil and Europe. The flight of directors and managers left the government so short of expertise that it could not adequately administer the state sector. The programme of nationalisation, like the programme of agrarian reform, had to be reversed in 1976. Socialist ministers replaced communist ones in the provisional revolutionary cabinets and appealed to the industrial families to return from Brazil and restore to Portugal the skills which only capitalism could provide in a country with a narrow base of education and experience.

The first sign that the extremists of the revolution were not going to carry all before them occurred on 25 April 1975. The militants in power celebrated this first anniversary of the April coup by holding elections for a constituent assembly to institutionalise the revolution and prepare a democratic constitution. When the votes were counted they were surprised that the extreme left, like the Christian right, was almost eclipsed by democratic socialists of various persuasions. The most prominent victor was Mário Soares, the son of a republican politician who had gained notoriety when Salazar had exiled him to the African island of São Tomé for having brought Portugal into disrepute by publicising abroad the moral hypocrisy of the old regime. The socialist victory was not enough to gain a grip on a government dominated by the military and Soares soon resigned the seat he was offered in cabinet as a token recognition of his political strength. He went further and led a huge demonstration through Lisbon protesting at alleged interference in the socialist press by communist shop stewards. As the military became more extreme in their agrarian and industrial interventions secret negotiations among politicians of the centre began to seek alternative options, even the possibility of an agreement between the Soares socialists and the now conservative exiles who surrounded Spínola. In the end, however, it was not the politicians who put an end to the governing alliance between

46   Colonel António Eanes (pronounced Yanesh) halted the
military and political extremism of late 1975 and was elected
state president in 1976. Farm workers at political rallies accepted his promise of stability with security.

communist civilians and armed forces captains but a moderate faction within the army. The end of extremism came on 25 November 1975 when António Ramalho Eanes, soon to be a general and
elected non-executive president of the republic, gained political ascendancy after a *coup d'état* that evicted the captains. Five months
later, on the second anniversary of the April revolt, Mário Soares
was elected to be the first democratic prime minister Portugal had
had for forty-nine years and eleven months.

While the two-year revolution evolved the world watched with
every shade of hope and anxiety. Diplomatic circles had been taken
completely by surprise at the fall of the oligarchy that had tried to
maintain the traditions of Salazar. The secret services were no better informed, and USA central intelligence appeared even to believe
its own propaganda that Portugal was winning the colonial war
in Mozambique. Financial circles, on the other hand, were expecting the change. Five days before the revolution western ministers
of finance meeting under the auspices of the prince-consort of The
Netherlands were briefed on the likelihood of a coup by a director

of the Lisbon shipyards who was intimate with Spínola. Two days later bankers dining at the Reform Club in London were interested in the impending collapse of colonial authority in Mozambique but predicted with what appeared to be astonishing and unruffled prescience that change would begin from Lisbon. When the change occurred the United States became concerned that one of its allies, with access to NATO military information, should have admitted a communist to its cabinet. The new government, rightly or wrongly, began to fear the possibility of United States interference of the kind witnessed in Latin America. The US ambassador, however, was a shrewd man who had lived through the Zanzibar revolution and later went on to become America's minister of defence. He apparently advised patient caution and in the climate of détente temporarily affecting Washington and Moscow no action was taken and the revolution burnt itself out as he had predicted. USA interference would probably have restored communist fortunes whereas the close affiliation of the Portuguese communist party to Moscow probably undermined appreciation of its political achievements. Communist public esteem peaked at 15 per cent of the popular vote before dwindling away.

The counter-coup which ended the revolution occurred, by coincidence or otherwise, a mere fortnight after the final winding up of the colonial empire. Deciding what to do about the colonial wars had been the first and most urgent policy decision to face the string of provisional cabinets which had tried to ride the revolution. The military decision was taken out of their hands when colonial conscripts, white and black, effectively refused to continue to fight for the empire. Where the African nationalist opponents were a clearly recognised force it was possible for cease-fires to be rapidly agreed and independence was promised to Guinea within weeks and to Mozambique within months. The transition was astonishingly peaceful after the years of bitter conflict, and social change was initially moderate and non-racial. In Angola the situation was more complex and the economic stakes were rather higher. Portugal tried to engineer a coalition of three predominantly African political parties which would form a government in which the settlers would hold the balance of power as a fourth force. This strategy failed and in July 1975 90 per cent of the settlers angrily fled, packing all that they could carry into containers and bitterly destroying much of what they left behind. They were replaced by three expeditionary armies called in by the three rival African political parties and a civil war fuelled by foreign intervention ensued. Portugal gave up trying to arbitrate and withdrew its last soldiers on 11 November 1975 under cover of darkness when the last proconsul in Africa announced that he was handing power not to one party but to 'the people of Angola as a whole'. Those of 'the people' who lived in the capital woke to find Zaire and South Africa pounding at the gates with heavy artillery and Cuban battalions defending it from the inside encouraged by a few thousand Portuguese who had stayed behind to support the 'popular' wing of the liberation movement.

One of the legacies of empire was the cosmopolitan population which flowed back to Portugal. Between the eighteenth century and the mid-twentieth century black people were rare in Lisbon and those who came were often a mixed-race colonial élite seeking university education or training at the school of colonial administration. In the 1970s migrants from the colonies were admitted in greater numbers, especially Cape Verdians who had been struck by the terrible Sahel droughts that affected their offshore islands. Economic refugees could not all reach the preferred destination among their relatives in the old whaling settlements of New England and so were allowed to sail to Portugal. There they replaced some of the migrants who had gone to France and sought employment niches as cheap casual labourers and domestics willing to live in tin shanties on the outskirts of Lisbon or in the dark tenements in the old city. With the collapse of the empire the Cape Verdians were joined in the loud and crowded urban slums and the peri-urban fishing villages by half a million returnees arriving suddenly by air in Europe's poorest if most scenic capital city. The often uneducated white returnees and black refugees were in competition with the indigenous poor in seeking meagre pickings as navvies mending mosaic pavements with little hammers. The younger returnees tried to liven the city up with the beat of modern African music that was to become popular across Europe.

The returning flotsam of empire accentuated an already severe social problem in the field of housing. In 1974 nearly 30 per cent of the population of Portugal lacked minimal housing of a decent standard. The economic expansion of the 1960s had brought an influx to the cities of Lisbon and Oporto and had turned the old fishing port of Setubal, south of Lisbon, into the nation's third largest urban complex. When the years of political silence ended local urban communities rapidly mobilised themselves to seek programmes of social renewal. Committees of residents adopted plans of action which sometimes cut across class cleavages in ways that neither industrial shop stewards nor agricultural labourers achieved. They aimed to control rents believing that ideally families should not pay more than 10 per cent of income on housing. To overcome the acute shortages they administered the occupation and distribution of vacant housing that had been abandoned by proprietors fleeing the revolution. The grass-roots politicians were encouraged by the armed forces movement and sought to usurp administrative roles that neither the city nor the state was able to fulfil. Street committees compaigned for improved health and child care and organised self-help programmes through 'dynamising' cells. Everyone had an opinion and took part in the endless discussions that became the basis of the new democracy. Such was the success of the open forum that differences were harmonised and guns were not used throughout the revolution.

After the revolution Portugal did not seriously aspire to restore its stake in Africa in the manner of the 'neo-colonial' French empire. A profound national amnesia cloaked almost everything to do with Africa, though a few business houses traded with Congo-Zaire and enterprising returnees who did not settle well in Portugal found a home in South Africa. Among the democratic leaders in Lisbon the socialists were disillusioned with their former African protégés and the captains of industry had their eyes firmly set on Europe. Only after a ten-year lapse did business-oriented government again take a hand in the politics of the ex-colonies. In Mozambique it was a Portuguese firm which was responsible for the management of the Zambezi hydro-electric scheme and Portugal therefore sought to end the wars of destabilisation, to rebuild the power lines to Pretoria, and to resume the garnering of revenues. The nationalist government of Mozambique gradually set aside its egalitarian ideals and made concessions to the foreign interests. In 1991 Portugal, with the support of Italy and the Vatican, brokered political compromises which brought about a ceasefire and opened the door to trade and investment in a Portuguese-speaking client republic. Rival British tycoons with stakes in the former Rhodesias and South Africa also aspired to a share of the spoils and during the new scramble to partition Africa economically Mozambique was incorporated into the British Commonwealth despite its tenacious preservation of Portuguese as the language of government and business.

Angola was a more attractive neo-colonial target than Mozambique but the competition there was even more intense. From the late 1980s the military defeat of South Africa on Angolan soil, the collapse of the Soviet Union as a major Cold War player in Africa, and the withdrawal of 40,000 Cuban soldiers and civil aid personnel, seemed to prepare the field for a return of the Portuguese. Many former Portuguese colonial settlers, officials and industrialists had hitherto expressed a strong preference for the ideology not of the government but of an opposition party which had abandoned its youthful Maoism to become the recipient of American arms in the first post-colonial civil war. More realistically, however, potential economic partners recognised that the oil wells, the urban administration, the Soviet-equipped air force and the bulging capital city with its dormant industrial capacity, were firmly in the hands of the quasi-Marxist government with which Portugal, though not the United States, had maintained correct if cold relations. The prospect of an end to the bitter conflicts between town and country, between pro-American and pro-Soviet factions, between the Portuguese-speaking middle class and the vernacular-speaking peasants and chiefs, led Angola's city-bred politicians to dream once more of the grandiose development projects which Portugal had abandoned in 1975. Plantations which had been scorched, mines which had been deserted, and irrigation dams which had been left unfinished appeared to retain their potential as Angola beckoned and Portugal aspired to bring peace and gain favoured access to both old and new resources of wealth. The first promising peace was brought about by a troika consisting of Russia, America and Portugal. This was followed by the country's first ever exercise in democratic politics and in 1992 the formerly Marxist ruling party won a parliamentary election orchestrated by the United Nations. The régime's heavily armed opponents refused to acknowledge their defeat, however, and Angola was plunged into two more civil wars.

Not until 2002 did a ferocious military tactic of starving the civilian populations of the remotest disaffected provinces lead to the cornering and killing of the rebel commander, Jonas Savimbi. Thereafter Portugal tried to use its diplomatic skills and linguistic advantages to out-manoeuvre French rivals and become Angola's bridgehead into a European Union keen to gain access to the former colony's off-shore oil wells and on-shore diamond fields.

After the revolution of 1974 the place of Portugal in the world was slowly seen to change. The country had begun its modern life in 1640 as a breakaway kingdom which rebelled against the union of the Iberian crowns. Thereafter a long search for economic viability had led to the building of two empires, one in America and the other in Africa, to three abortive attempts at industrialisation in the late seventeenth, late eighteenth and late nineteenth centuries, and to a close association with Britain in order to guarantee an outlet for Portugal's quality wine. In the 1980s the scene changed completely. The American empire in Brazil was largely forgotten, though the advent of television brought a flood of Brazilian video-dramas to Portuguese screens. Africa was at least temporarily eclipsed though it continued to feature on television news as the post-colonial wars dragged on. For most Portuguese, African reality hardly impinged on political life and the generations which had served in the bush war put their memories behind them with suppressed bitterness while the young claimed to know nothing of the recent colonial past. The old economists who had tried to industrialise Portugal in past centuries became popular subjects of analysis by academic historians, but the industries of the mid-twentieth century were often multinational in structure and not therefore a source of domestic pride. The British survived in folk memory as the arrogant, quasi-colonial, foreign gentry to whom a semi-mocking deference had been due, but the pervasive British influence over trade and technology vanished as the metric system replaced the pound and the square inch. The greatest change, however, after three and a half centuries of fiercely proclaimed independence, was the restoration of closer ties with Spain.

It might have been expected that ties between Portugal and Spain would have been restored when both countries were ruled by dictators cautiously sympathetic to the fascist powers of the 1930s. This did not happen, although Salazar did help Franco to win the civil war and Franco did not look too closely when refugees sent from Lisbon to Madrid for exemplary punishment included a few smuggled Portuguese whom Salazar had found to be uncomfortably recalcitrant. Both dictators, however, were primarily nationalists and it was left to their successors, social democrats and democratic socialists, to restore cooperation if not friendship. New Iberian free trade arrangements led Spain's trade with Portugal to exceed its trade with the former Spanish American empire while Portugal's trade with Spain began to exceed its dealings with Britain. Spain also began to invest in Portugal after 1985 and soon more capital was going there than into any other foreign country. Spanish tourists were attracted by low Portuguese prices and outnumbered all other tourists put together. Although the Portuguese began to rival the British as visitors to Spain a trade gap of a billion dollars nevertheless opened up between the neighbouring Iberian nations. It was hoped that closer links would be mutually beneficial and plans were even made to link the booming southern cities of Andalusia to Portugal with a highway. The flow of people and goods, however, was exceeded by the flow of Spanish capital as Spanish firms sought to benefit from Portuguese wages that were only half the ones they paid at home. Portuguese banks, restored to their private owners after the revolution had died down, faced a new threat from invading Spanish banks, and in the new climate old disputes over fishing grounds and textile tariffs had to be resolved. Finally the Spanish king, who had spent his childhood exile in Portugal, was able to return for a state visit and admired the great abbey of Batalha, a symbol of nationhood which the Portuguese had built six hundred years before to commemorate their defeat of the Castilian aspiration to unify Iberia in 1385.

New relations with its nearest neighbour were only one of the transitions of the 1980s. A small hiccup occurred in 1983 when a conservative administration broke up after the accidental death of its leader, but a return to socialist leadership brought none of the old fire of the revolution. Radical soldiers had virtually gone from politics and the majority of the Portuguese workforce had opted to join non-communist trade unions which accepted periodic belt-tightening with reasonable equanimity. The most prominent year of change in post-revolutionary Portugal was 1986. It marked the end of ten years of 'probationary' democracy during which a conservative segment of the army's officer corps had kept a watching brief over the politicians. The colonel who had led the counter-coup of 1975, António Eanes, completed his second five-year term as the elected president of the second republic. The revolutionary council which had grown out of the radical military tradition of 1974 was wound up and civilian rule became entrenched. The new president elected in 1986 was the veteran democratic socialist, Mário Soares, who defeated his conservative rival and became a non-partisan president for all the people of Portugal. So popular and trusted a figure did Soares prove to be, after his long survival as the voice of democracy under the old dictatorship, and after his skilled ministerial apprenticeship weaving a middle way between the factions of anarchists, communists, militarists and former fascists, that in 1991 he was re-elected to a second presidential term with acclaim.

On the parliamentary scene 1986 was also a year of change. A few months earlier an abrasive young economist, Cavaco Silva, had been elected to the office of prime minister. Cavaco had been trained in Britain in the Thatcher mould and his ascendancy marked out a new direction for Portugal. Socialist and semi-socialist policies which had partially eradicated the inhuman harshness of the later Salazar years and of Caetano's last fling were now replaced by a fashionable European conservatism. The new ideologues believed that business, rather than the state, would be the most reliable purveyor of the services which Portugal had lacked for so long. Not only were banks and state industries denationalised but public service utilities, which had never before been in private hands, were sold off to an entrepreneurial élite which was once more restored to favour. Cavaco rode a wave of economic growth which so masked some of the economic pains of change that he was able to win two more general elections, the first-ever prime minister of Portugal to be given a parliamentary majority. His cohabitation with the old socialist president brought a decade of political stability, underpinned it has to be said by 700 tons of gold reserves which the 'fascists' had built up during the decades of austerity and which the 'socialists' had refrained from syphoning off to finance their experiments in social and political reconstruction.

The year 1986 brought in not only a new civilian president and a new conservative prime minister, but also a new set of economic challenges and opportunities. While the empire went through its post-colonial death throes Portugal took stock of itself in the aftermath of its own revolution. Having turned its back on the old Africa in the mid-1970s it sought instead to come to terms with the new Europe. An application to join the European 'community' had been made by the socialist governments of the late 1970s. The tough negotiations were undertaken by the conservative governments of the early 1980s led by rehabilitated politicians who had served as a small 'liberal' faction in the last 'parliament' of the pre-revolutionary regime. Entering Europe in 1986 was seen as gaining a badge of democratic respectability as well as opening new economic doors. Brussels did not anticipate that Portugal would be a difficult country to swallow since the entire Portuguese domestic product amounted to only one per cent of Europe's total product, though Portugal did offer some competition in the sensitive Mediterranean farm sector. In agriculture the greatest change which new freedoms brought to rural Portugal was the evolution of producer cooperatives, particularly in the wine industry. Farmers who had previously been dependent for their outlets on exploitative private entrepreneurs now acquired socially responsible marketing systems backed by government-sponsored agricultural extension programmes. The quality of Portuguese wine rose in tandem with a small increase in peasant well-being. The national product of an average Portuguese, although only half that of an average Spaniard, and one third of that of an average European, rose towards 5000 US dollars a year during the 1980s, ten times the 500 dollars per capita per annum of the painful post-war years.

Entry into the European Economic Community (soon to become the European Union) was achieved in 1986. Integration coincided with an economic boom which lasted for nearly a decade and brought a number of visible changes to the face of Portugal. The country's first thousand miles of motorway transformed a transport infrastructure that had previously relied on creaking railways and cobbled roads. The chief beneficiaries of European modernisation were people in the coastal towns rather than the half-neglected population of the hills and backlands. The cities skipped with alacrity from the age of the electric tram to that of the motor car without adopting either Dutch-style bicycles or Italian-style motor-scooters. As cities became choked by the motor revolution Volkswagen built a factory with a massive billion-euro subsidy from the European Union. The good years were also fuelled by the absorption into the labour market of the half-million colonial settlers and military conscripts who returned from Africa to find jobs in the burgeoning services and in the construction industry. One dramatic symbol of change was the opening of Europe's largest copper mine, but by the time production reached 150,000 tonnes commodity prices had weakened and Portugal's European honeymoon was over.

The mid-1990s saw the end of the transitional fiscal privileges which Portugal had enjoyed along with other late entrants to Europe from the Mediterranean. Visible changes in infrastructure had not been matched by any radical improvements in economic structure. Although growth rates had temporarily been high, Portugal was never able to match France in tapping into the huge bounty which the European Union spent on subsiding agriculture. Portugal's farming industry declined steeply. In 1960 a quarter of Portugal's national product had been derived from farming and fishing, but by 2000 obsolete patterns of land tenure, archaic methods of farm production and an uneconomic fleet of small fishing boats had reduced Portugal's traditional industries to less than four per cent of national production. Some growth occurred in forestry where the great cork and pine forests were supplemented by the planting of half a million hectares of eucalyptus trees. Farmers on the other hand produced less than half of Portugal's food and even animal fodder had to be supplemented with imports. Meanwhile the tourist industry, catering to day-trippers from Spain and to some of the four million overseas Portuguese who took their holidays back home, surpassed agriculture as a source of revenue and as an employer of labour. On the southern beaches of the Algarve tourism also welcomed a million-odd British and other northern visitors. By the beginning of the twenty-first century some up-market tourist developments were adding commercial value to Portugal's rich artistic and architectural heritage. Despite the shift from agriculture to service industries Portuguese salaries languished and the average hourly wage remained a mere seven euros compared to a European average of twenty-one euros. The average national wealth remained at half that of Ireland though low prices gave the Portuguese a somewhat less depressed purchasing power.

Poverty among producers was matched by low productivity among service providers and the heady initial days of European integration did not lead to any rapid improvement in the human development index. In 1991 official statistics recognised that at least 200,000 children were known to be working full adult hours, losing out on education without earning adult rates of pay. Over the next ten years half of all Portuguese children continued to leave school at the age of fourteen. Indices of health among these children (and indeed among their parents) lagged far behind those of other western countries even though infant mortality was reduced from ten per thousand to five per thousand. Adolescents who did complete secondary school were sometimes forced to look to the private sector for further training and one third of all Portugal's university students were enrolled in independent colleges. When dismay at the lack of health and educational facilities was compounded by an economic down-turn the electorate finally rejected the conservatives and returned the socialists to power in 1995. Managing structural change during a recession was no easy task, however, and even a government willing to enhance spending could not compensate for Portugal's inefficient work practices in over-staffed bureaucracies. The tide turned once more in 2002 and a new conservative government promised to tackle the crisis in health provision, if necessary by selling hospitals off to the profit-making sector of the economy.

While governments struggled to enhance economic production and to economise on tax-based social services, Portugal went through a period of national soul searching. Entry into the European Union had, in effect, taken away the boundaries of the nation which had stood for eight centuries. Spain, which according to one humorist had always viewed Portugal as an anachronism comparable to Gibraltar, continued to take advantage of the now open border. Portugal's fragmented investment structure attracted foreigners to buy into real estate as well as into the financial sector. Low rates of pay, however, did not significantly attract investment into productive enterprises and low-cost international manufacturing and assembling continued to move away from the Mediterranean rim and towards Asia. In the case of Portugal's key textile, clothing and footwear sectors the fall of the Iron Curtain opened up fierce competition from eastern European factories which were conveniently placed to supply the great consumer markets of Germany. In order to defend the national identity of Portugal, and to publicise the modernity of its economy, a world trade fair was hosted by Lisbon in 1998. The fair brought urban renewal to the northern suburbs and coincided with the opening of the new bridge across the Tagus which linked the city to its far-flung industrial suburbs in the east. Nearly two million of Portugal's ten million people now lived in and around the metropolis. Although many were poor they now lived in a modern democracy and many had acquired an urban cultural outlook similar to that of the diaspora Portuguese scattered across western Europe. Back in the rural provinces, however, Portugal still retained a distinctive peasant vitality which was all its own. Families remained strong and coherent although work on the land was still hard. During their great reunions the clans enjoyed the unique Portuguese cuisine of mixed fish stews, barbecued goat's meat and strong red wine. The colourful romance of traditional festivals was enriched on high days and holidays by the visits of friends and family who earned their money abroad. Portuguese culture and custom remained vibrant in the twenty-first century.

HOUSES OF AVIS, BEJA AND HABSBURG

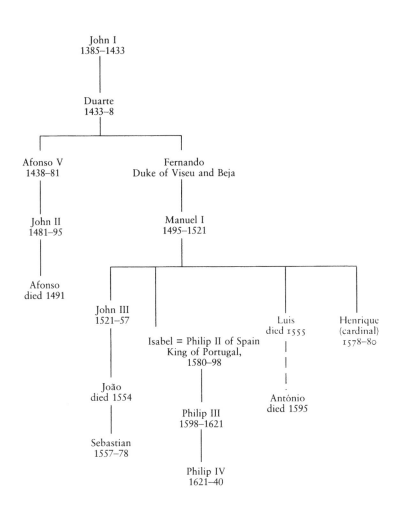

John I
1385–1433

Duarte
1433–8

Afonso V
1438–81

Fernando
Duke of Viseu and Beja

John II
1481–95

Manuel I
1495–1521

Afonso
died 1491

John III
1521–57

Luis
died 1555

Henrique
(cardinal)
1578–80

Isabel = Philip II of Spain
King of Portugal,
1580–98

João
died 1554

António
died 1595

Philip III
1598–1621

Sebastian
1557–78

Philip IV
1621–40

HOUSES OF BRAGANZA AND BRAGANZA-SAXE-COBURG

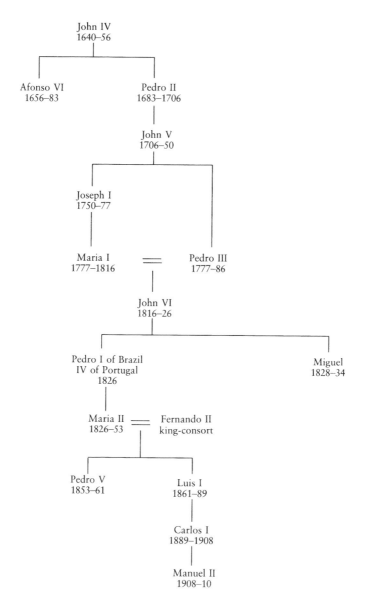

John IV
1640–56

Afonso VI
1656–83

Pedro II
1683–1706

John V
1706–50

Joseph I
1750–77

Maria I
1777–1816

Pedro III
1777–86

John VI
1816–26

Pedro I of Brazil
IV of Portugal
1826

Miguel
1828–34

Maria II
1826–53

Fernando II
king-consort

Pedro V
1853–61

Luis I
1861–89

Carlos I
1889–1908

Manuel II
1908–10

REPUBLICAN PRESIDENTS

Teófilo Braga	1910–11, 1915
Manuel de Arriaga	1911–15
Bernardino Guimarães	1915–17, 1925–6
Sidónio Pais	1917–18
João Antunes	1918–19
António de Almeida	1919–23
Manuel Teixeira Gomes	1923–5
Oscar Carmona (prime minister, then president)	1926–51
[António Salazar (president of the Council of Ministers)	1932–68]
Craveiro Lopes	1951–8
Américo Thómas	1958–74
[Marcello Caetano (president of the Council of Ministers)	1968–74]
António Spínola	1974
Francisco da Costa Gomes	1974–6
António Ramalho Eanes	1976–86
Mário Soares	1986–96
[Anibal Cavaco Silva (prime minister)	1985–95]
Jorge Sampaio	1996–
[António Guterres (prime minister)	1995–2002
José Durão Barroso	2002–]

SELECT SOURCE MATERIALS

José Hermano Saraiva, *História de Portugal* (6 vols., Publicaçoes Alfa, Lisbon, 1983–84, illustrated)

V. Magalhães Godinho, *Os Descobrimentos e a Economia Mundial* (4 vols., second edition, Presença, Lisbon, 1981)

F. Mauro, *Le Portugal et l'Atlantique au XVIIe siècle* (Ecole Pratique des Hautes Etudes, Paris, 1960)

Flausino Torres, *Portugal: Uma Perspectiva da sua História* (Afrontamento, Oporto, n. d.)

Susan Schneider, *O Marquês de Pombal e o Vinho do Porto* (Regra do Jogo, Lisbon, 1980)

Teresa Bernardino, *Sociedade e Atitudes Mentais em Portugal 1777–1810* (Imprensa Nacional, Lisbon, 1986)

V. Magalhães Godinho, *A Estrutura da Antiga Sociedade Portuguesa* (second edition, Lisbon, 1975)

Manuel Villaverde Cabral, *O Desenvolvimento do Capitalismo em Portugal no século XIX* (Regra do Jogo, Lisbon, 1981)

Miriam Halpern Pereira, Maria de Fátima Sá e Melo Ferreira and João B. Serra, *O Liberalismo na Península Ibérica* (2 vols., Sá da Costa, Lisbon, 1982)

Manuel Villaverde Cabral, *Portugal na Alvorada do Século XX* (Regra do Jogo, Lisbon, 1979)

Jaime Reis, Maria Filomena Mónica and Maria de Lourdes Lima dos Santos, *O Século XIX em Portugal* (Presença, Lisbon, n. d.)

Vasco Pulido Valente, *O Poder e o Povo* (Dom Quixote, Lisbon, 1974)

António José Telo, *O Sidonismo e o Movimento Operário Português* (Biblioteca Ulmeiro, Lisbon, n. d.)

José António Saraiva and Júlio Henriques, *O 28 de Maio e o Fim do Liberalismo* (2 vols., Bertrand, Lisbon, 1978)

Oliveira Martins, *Portugal Contemporâneo* (2 vols., third edition 1984, reprinted Lello e Irmão, Lisbon, 1981)

Franco Nogueira, *Salazar: Estudo Biográfico* (Atlântida Editora, Coimbra, and Livraria Civilização, Oporto, 6 vols., 1977–85)

Jacques Georgel, *Le Salazarisme: Histoire et Bilan 1926–1974* (Cujas, Paris, 1981)

António Barreto, *Memória da Reforma Agrária* (Publicações Europa-America, Lisbon, n. d.)

J. Rentes de Carvalho, *Portugal, de Bloem en de Sikkel* (Arbeiderspers, Amsterdam, 1975)

Mario Filomena Mónica, *Os Grandes Patrões da Indústria Portuguesa* (Dom Quixote, Lisbon, 1990)

Joaquim Veríssimo Serrão, *História de Portugal* (Verbo, Lisbon, in progress)

Valentim Alexandre, *Origens do Colonialismo Português Moderno* (Sá da Costa, Lisbon, 1979)

Maria Filomena Mónica, *O Movimento Socialista em Portugal* (Imprensa Nacional, Lisbon, 1985)

António M. Hespanha, *As Vésperas do Leviathan* (Rio do Mouro, Ferreira, 1987)

António José Telo, *Portugal na Segunda Guerra* (P & R, Lisbon, 1987)

António José Telo, *Decadência e Queda da I República Portuguesa* (Regra do Jogo, Lisbon, 1980)

Albert Silbert, *Le Portugal Méditerranéen à la Fin de l'Ancien Régime* (3 vols., INIC, Lisbon, 1978)

Manuel Braga da Cruz, *O Partido e o Estado no Salazarismo* (Presença, Lisbon, 1988)

César Oliveira, *Portugal e a II República de Espanha* (P & R, Lisbon, n. d.)

César Oliveira, *Salazar e a Guerra Civil de Espanha* (O Jornal, Lisbon, 1987)

Sebastião José de Carvalho e Melo, *Escritos Económicos de Londres 1741–1747* (Biblioteca Nacional, Lisbon, 1986)

João Medina, *Oh a República* (INIC, Lisbon, 1990)

David Justino, *A Formação do Espaço Económico Nacional Português 1810–1913* (2 vols., Vega, Lisbon, 1989)

Manuel Villaverde Cabral, *O Operariado nas Vésperas da República* (Presença, Lisbon, 1977)

J. Borges de Macedo, *Problemas de História da Indústria Portuguesa no Século XVIII* (second edition, Querco, Lisbon, 1982)

Suzanne Chantal, *La vie Quotidienne au Portugal après le Tremblement de Terre de Lisbonne de 1755* (Hachette, Paris, 1960)

Eça de Queirós, *Os Maias* (Biblioteca Ulisseia, Lisbon, fourth edition, 1988, fiction, first published 1888)

Pepetela [Artur Pestana], *Yaka* (Publicações Dom Quixote, Lisbon, second edition, 1985, fiction)

SELECTED WORKS PUBLISHED
SINCE 1990

A Monarquia Feudal 1096–1480 by José Mattoso and Armindo de Sousa (Estampa, Lisbon, 1993) is the second volume of the monumental *História de Portugal* commissioned by José Mattoso. It contains his own illuminating reassessment of the social and cultural history of the Portuguese middle ages. For an extensive bibliography of historical works on Portugal, and a comprehensive index of people and topics, see volume eight of the Mattoso set.

Jorge de Almeida and Maria de Albuquerque have written a graphic study, *Os Panéis de Nuno Gonçalves* (Verbo, Lisbon, 2000), which decodes the symbolism of the double triptych of the Portuguese court and its retainers mourning the martyrdom of Prince Fernando. The display shows two pictures of the beatified prince who had been left in Morocco as a hostage by his brother Henry and who was subsequently killed in 1443 when he ceased to have any value as a hostage. The authors authenticate the attribution of the painting to Nuno Gonçalves while convincingly suggesting that the work was commissioned in 1445, a surprisingly early date subsequently made more plausible by dendrochronological counts on the six panels of Baltic oak.

Prince Henry 'the Navigator' A Life (Yale, New Haven, 2000) is the culmination of a life's work by an Oxford scholar, Peter Russell, who quietly unravelled the patriotic mythologies surrounding the 'Lancastrian' Portuguese prince and wrote an outstanding alternative account of fifteenth-century Portugal and its overseas aspirations.

Luis Vaz de Camões: The Lusiads (Oxford University Press, 1997) is a prize-winning poetic translation of the great Camões epic of empire by one of the leading historians of the Portuguese empire, Landeg White, who is also a published poet in his own right.

David Birmingham's *Trade and Empire in the Atlantic 1400–1600* (Routledge, London, 2000) is for those who like their history succinct but felt that Cambridge's concise history of Portugal was just too concise on the history of the Atlantic empire.

The Portuguese Empire in Asia 1500–1700: a political and economic history (Longman, London, 1993) by Sanjay Subrahmanyam is one of the most ambitious and richly documented pieces of revisionist Portuguese history and puts the Oriental branch of the empire into a broad context of Asian history hitherto scarcely visible from the Lisbon perspective. The author has also published *The career and legend of Vasco da Gama* (Cambridge University Press, 1998).

James D. Tracy has edited *The Political Economy of Merchant Empires: State Power and World Trade 1350–1750* (Cambridge University Press, 1991), a sequel to his volume on the rise of merchant empires. He asks fundamentally new questions about the economic aspects of empires and thus sheds much new light on the Portuguese in the widest possible context.

Renascent Empire? The House of Braganza and the Quest for Stability in Monsoon Asia ca. 1640–1683 (Amsterdam University Press, 2000) by Glenn J. Ames is a well-researched study of the seventeenth-century rise of the House of Braganza during the twilight years of the Asian empire.

Angela Delaforce explores the artistic and musical consequences of the wealth which Portugal derived from its eighteenth-century Brazilian empire in her richly illustrated book *Art and Patronage in Eighteenth-Century Portugal* (Cambridge University Press, 2002). She thus makes good some of the serious deficiencies in cultural history which readers noted in the present concise study.

Kenneth Maxwell pursues and illustrates the reassessment of Pombal from a cruel dictator to a rather more visionary politician steeped in scholarly reading in *Pombal: Paradox of the Enlightenment* (Cambridge University Press, 1995).

Dauril Alden, America's leading specialist on Brazil, has written *The Making of an Enterprise: The Society of Jesus in Portugal, its Empire and Beyond, 1540–1750* (Stanford University Press, 1996) a monumental study of the Portuguese Jesuits. The book is dedicated to Charles Boxer, a British scholar to whom Alden subsequently devoted a biography.

O Império Luso-Brasileiro (Estampa, Lisbon, 1986, 1991, 1992) consists of a three-part comprehensive survey of colonial Brazil in the Joel Serrão and Oliveira Marques eleven-volume *Nova História da Expansão Portuguesa*. Part one was edited by Harold Johnson and Maria Beatriz Nizza da Silva, part two by Frédéric Mauro and part three again by Maria Beatriz Nizza da Silva.

O Liberalismo (Estampa, Lisbon, 1993) edited by Luís Torgal and João Roque is the fifth volume of the José Mattoso *História de Portugal*. It is a radical appraisal of the historiography of the Liberalism and Republicanism which had been so persistently and comprehensively denigrated by scholars funded and encouraged by the dictatorship of 1926 to 1974.

Os Sons do Silêncio: o Portugal de Oitocentos e a Abolição do Tráfico de Escravos (Imprensa de Ciências Sociais, Lisbon, 1999) or 'the sounds of silence' is the ironic title of a work by João Pedro Marques on the Portuguese campaign against the slave trade. The book highlights the importance of the debate between the radicals of the September revolution, who won ill-deserved credit for abolition, and their pragmatic opponents, who saw the benefits of permitting the trade to be suppressed by the British.

Portugal e O Estado Novo (1930–1960) (Presença, Lisbon, 1990) edited by Fernando Rosas is the twelfth volume of the Joel Serrão and Oliveira Marques *Nova História de Portugal* and consists of essays collated by the leading modern scholar of the Salazar era. Subsequent writings by Fernando Rosas present the period with a growing depth of perception and perspective.

O Estado Novo e a Igreja Católica (Bizâncio, Lisbon, 1998) by Manuel Braga da Cruz, explores the tortured relations of Salazar's overtly Catholic dictatorship with the Vatican and the Portuguese priesthood.

Politics in the Portuguese Empire: The State, Industry and Cotton, 1926–1974 (Clarendon Press, Oxford, 1993) by Anne Pitcher carefully assesses the myth and the reality in Salazar's relations with his African empire in the context of the potentially important textile industry.

O Império Africano (Estampa, Lisbon, 1998, 2001) consists of two parts of the Joel Serrão and Oliveira Marques series on empire. It sheds light on post-imperial researches undertaken not only in Portugal but also in Africa itself and in the wider world. The period 1825 to 1890 is edited by Valentim Alexandre and Jill Dias and the period 1890 to 1930 by Oliveira Marques.

Lusotropicalisme: Idéologies coloniales et identités nationales dans les mondes lusophones (Karthala, Paris, 1997) is one of the massive volumes of international work collected and edited under the annual title *Lusotopie* by French scholars led by Michel Cahen. The tomes are devoted to all Portuguese-speaking countries, including Timor, and to all themes, including religious studies.

"O Modo Português de estar no Mundo" O luso-tropicalismo e a ideologia colonial portuguesa (1933–1961) (Afrontamento, Oporto, 1999) by Cláudia Castelo is a succinct revisionist essay on the once fashionable theories of Portuguese racial tolerance.

A Geração da Utopia (Dom Quixote, Lisbon, 1992) by Pepetela captures the flavour of the late empire through the eyes of fictional African students in Lisbon and poignantly follows their illusions and disillusions. It is one of several highly acclaimed novels by Pepetela which reflect Portuguese experience in Angola from the seventeenth century to the present.

Marion Kaplan has written a historical survey, *The Portuguese: the Land and its People* (Penguin, London, 1991) which nicely complements the Cambridge history and includes a good discussion of literature and the arts.

Kenneth Maxwell, the biographer of Pombal, has written a most scholarly and dispassionate international analysis of the revolution of 1974, *The Making of Portuguese Democracy* (Cambridge University Press, 1995). It includes such gems as an American reference to the young António Eanes as our 'boyscout for democracy' when he was sent for training at NATO headquarters.

Patrick Chabal and others have written *A History of Postcolonial Lusophone Africa* (Hurst, London, 2002) including surveys of postcolonial Mozambique by Malyn Newitt and of Angola by David Birmingham. The book is a sequel to Chabal's *The Postcolonial Literature of Lusophone Africa* (Hurst, London, 1998).

Karl Maier, a brilliant American journalist, captures the legacy of empire in *Angola: Promises and Lies* (Serif, London, 1996).

David Mourão-Ferreira's highly acclaimed work of fiction, *Um Amor Feliz* (Presença, Lisbon, 1986), tells more about society and social relations in Portugal than most academic works of social science.

Claudine Roulet's prize-winning novel in French, *Rien qu'une écaille* (Monographic, Sierre, 1996), captures the subtle flavour of late Portuguese 'fascism' from the perspective of a woman surveying her life while living temporarily on the Azores islands.

David Birmingham, *Portugal e África* (Vega, Lisbon, 2003) essays on the Portuguese in Africa translated by Arlindo Barbeitos and published in English by Ohio University Press, Athens, 2004.

Jean-François Labourdette, *História de Portugal* (Dom Quixote, Lisbon, 2001, originally in French, 2000).

FURTHER READING IN ENGLISH

A. H. de Oliveira Marques, *History of Portugal* (2 vols., Columbia University Press, New York, 1972)

C. R. Boxer, *The Portuguese Seaborne Empire* (Hutchinson, London, 1969)

José Cutileiro, *A Portuguese Rural Society* (Clarendon Press, Oxford, 1971)

Rose Macaulay, *They Went to Portugal* (Jonathan Cape, London, 1946)

Rose Macaulay, *They Went to Portugal Too* (Carcanet, Manchester, 1990)

A. C. de C. M. Saunders, *A Social History of Black Slaves and Freedmen in Portugal* (Cambridge University Press, Cambridge, 1982)

Carl A. Hanson, *Economy and Society in Baroque Portugal* (Macmillan, London, 1981)

Kenneth Maxwell, *Conflicts and Conspiracies: Brazil and Portugal* (Cambridge University Press, Cambridge, 1973)

R. F. Disney, *The Twilight of the Pepper Empire* (Harvard Press, Cambridge, Mass., 1978)

Stanley Paine, *A History of Spain and Portugal* (2 vols., Wisconsin University Press, Madison, 1973)

C. R. Boxer, *Race Relations in the Portuguese Colonial Empire* (Oxford University Press, London, 1963)

H. V. Livermore, *A New History of Portugal* (Cambridge University Press, Cambridge, 1977)

C. R. Boxer, *The Golden Age of Brazil* (University of California Press, Berkeley, 1966)

Joseph C. Miller, *Way of Death: Merchant Capitalism and the Angolan Slave Trade* (Wisconsin University Press, Madison, and James Currey, London, 1989)

A. D. Francis, *The Methuens of Portugal* (Cambridge University Press, Cambridge, 1977)

C. R. Boxer, *Salvador de Sá and the Struggle for Brazil and Angola* (Athlone Press, London, 1952)

H. E. S. Fisher, *The Portugal Trade: A Study in Anglo-Portuguese Commerce* (Methuen, London, 1971)

L. M. E. Shaw, *Trade, Inquisition and the English Nation in Portugal* (Carcanet, Manchester, 1989)

Sandro Sideri, *Trade and Power: Informal Colonialism in Anglo-Portuguese Relations* (Rotterdam University Press, Rotterdam, 1970)

Gervase Clarence-Smith, *The Third Portuguese Empire* (Manchester University Press, Manchester, 1985)

Richard Hammond, *Portugal and Africa 1815–1910* (Stanford University Press, Stanford, 1966)

Douglas Wheeler, *Republican Portugal* (Wisconsin University Press, Madison, 1975)

Tom Gallagher, *Portugal: A Twentieth-Century Interpretation* (Manchester University Press, Manchester, 1983)

Richard Robinson, *Contemporary Portugal* (Allen and Unwin, London, 1979)

Hugh Kay, *Salazar and Modern Portugal* (Eyre and Spottiswoode, London, 1970)

John Sykes, *Portugal and Africa: the People and the War* (Hutchinson, London, 1971)

António de Figueiredo, *Portugal: Fifty Years of Dictatorship* (Holmes and Meier, New York, and Penguin, Harmondsworth, 1976)

T. D. Hendrick, *The Lisbon Earthquake* (London, 1956)

D. L. Raby, *Fascism and Resistance in Portugal* (Manchester University Press, Manchester, 1988)

Lawrence S. Graham and Douglas L. Wheeler, *In Search of Modern Portugal: the Revolution and its Consequences* (Wisconsin University Press, Madison, 1983)

A. J. R. Russell-Wood, *A World on the Move: the Portuguese in Africa, Asia and America 1415–1808* (Carcanet, Manchester, 1992)

Bruce Chatwin, *The Viceroy of Ouidah* (Jonathan Cape, London, 1980, fiction)

José Saramago, *The Year of the Death of Ricardo Reis* (Harper Collins, London, 1992, fiction)

David Birmingham, *Frontline Nationalism in Angola and Mozambique* (James Currey, London, 1992)

INDEX

Page numbers in italic refer to illustrations